The Carbohydrate Craver's Diet

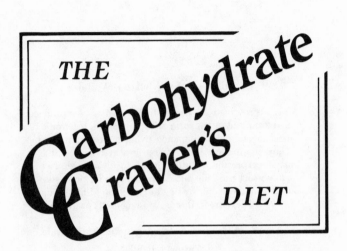

THE Carbohydrate Craver's DIET

Judith J. Wurtman, Ph.D.

HOUGHTON MIFFLIN COMPANY · BOSTON

Library of Congress Cataloging in Publication Data

Wurtman, Judith J.
The carbohydrate craver's diet.

Includes index.
1. Low-calorie diet.   2. High-carbohydrate diet.
3. Low-calorie diet—Recipes.   4. High-carbohydrate
diet—Recipes.   I. Title.
RM222.2.W87   1983   613.2′5   82-15545
ISBN 0-395-33160-9

Printed in the United States of America

S 10 9 8 7 6 5 4 3 2

The author is grateful for permission to reprint from the following:
"Nutrients that Modify Brain Function," by Richard J. Wurtman.
Copyright © 1982 by Scientific American, Inc. All rights reserved.
"Carbohydrate Craving in Obese People," by Judith J. Wurtman, et al.
First published in the *International Journal of Eating Disorders* 1:1
(1981). The desirable weight tables are reprinted courtesy of Metropol-
itan Life Insurance Company.

To my children,
Rachael Elisabeth
and David Franklin

Acknowledgments

THIS BOOK could not have been written without the invaluable help and support of my editor, Frances Tenenbaum. Her constant encouragement, her searching questions when something was not entirely clear, her superb ability to organize and edit, gave shape and clarity to the book. She is a rare individual and a gift to any writer.

The diets were developed, in large part, by the meticulous care of my good friend and MIT colleague Rita Tsay. Her attention to grams and calories ensured that the food lists, menus, and recipes would provide nutritional completeness and her imagination helped develop the varied meal plans. She was even willing to time the preparation of the Super Salads to make sure it could be done on a busy schedule.

I want to express my special gratitude to Helen Rees, my agent. Her unfailing belief in the book and her uncanny sense of how to encourage me during the long process of writing contributed in large part to the pleasure I had in writing it. We

vii

started out our relationship as author and agent; we continue it as close friends.

But it is to my husband that I must acknowledge the most gratitude. Our research collaborations for many years produced the scientific information on which the Carbohydrate Craver's Diet is based, and his persistent search for the most scientifically valid answers makes this information honest and creditable. Moreover, our sojourn in Switzerland last year, while he was a visiting professor at the University of Geneva, gave me the leisure to start the book amidst the glories of Swiss Alps and chocolate. And finally, his unfailing belief that this book would be done made it so.

Contents

The
Carbohydrate
Craver's
Diet

1

The Carbohydrate Connection

"I never thought I could satisfy my
need to eat sweets with less than a bag
of cookies or half a chocolate cake. I
never believed it could be done. But
now I have a tiny candy bar every
night and I'm satisfied. And for the first
time, I'm finally actually losing
weight."

— *A patient*

PEOPLE, RATS, and many other animals have a
specific hunger for carbohydrates — sweets and
starches — that cannot be satisfied by eating any
other kind of food. After a big meal, you may
blanch at the thought of another bite of steak, but
you'll still be "hungry" for dessert. Your stomach
will be stuffed with three servings of salad at lunch,
but you will feel unsatisfied because you haven't
met your body's need for a carbohydrate-rich food.
And between meals, when you get the urge to eat
something, that something is likely to be a package

1

of cookies, a candy bar, crackers, or ice cream.

Individuals have different degrees of carbohydrate hunger just as individuals need different amounts of sleep. There are people who really don't like bread and desserts, just as there are people who get by on three hours of sleep every night. In fact, most people who have no weight problem are probably not aware of a hunger for carbohydrates. They routinely satisfy it by eating starchy foods with their meals and by snacking on carbohydrate foods when they feel like eating something between meals.

The overweight person is acutely aware of a craving for carbohydrate because for years sweets and starches have been forbidden foods. And this craving is intensified on a high-protein–low-carbohydrate diet. The carbohydrate craver will almost inevitably fail on such a diet, not because of weakness of will power or moral fiber but because the body's real hunger for carbohydrates isn't met by these diets.

If you are a carbohydrate craver, you know only too well what happens. You manage to deprive yourself of carbohydrates for just so long, and then your craving becomes so intense that you break down and eat something: perhaps a candy bar or a few crackers or a doughnut. Then you find you cannot stop. As one of my patients who had been on a high-protein–low-carbohydrate diet explained, "It's as if there is a demon inside me saying, 'Eat more, more, more.'"

So you begin to binge on carbohydrates, and as you put back the pounds you so painfully lost, you also fill with guilt at having failed still another diet. Yet the fact is, as we have shown in the laboratory, *there is no way that the true carbohydrate craver can succeed on a high-protein–low-carbohydrate diet.*

For years scientists have been aware of anecdotal evidence for a carbohydrate hunger, but they assumed it was the same thing as a general need for food. They linked it with a drop in blood sugar levels and thought that the body was simply running out of energy. If you persisted in believing that this carbohydrate hunger could be satisfied only with a sweet or starchy food, they said you had an overactive sweet tooth or blamed it on your childhood upbringing — a mother who rewarded you with cookies or punished you by taking away dessert. In any event, according to their reasoning, the problem was not your body, but your emotions.

But they are wrong. My colleagues and I in our laboratory at the Department of Nutrition and Food Sciences at the Massachusetts Institute of Technology have shown that a carbohydrate hunger actually exists. And we have proved that this hunger comes not from an emotional need to eat sweet or starchy foods but from a very specific metabolic need.

My interest in the existence of a carbohydrate hunger goes back several years. About ten years ago, others at MIT had shown that the manufacture of a brain chemical, serotonin, is influenced by the amount of carbohydrate-rich foods an animal or a human eats. Serotonin, one of a class of brain chemicals known as neurotransmitters, is made from tryptophan, an amino acid. (Amino acids are the components of protein.) When carbohydrate foods are eaten, insulin is released into the blood. Insulin increases the amount of tryptophan that gets into the brain and, subsequently, the level and activity of serotonin. When enough serotonin is produced in the brain, it turns off the hunger for carbohydrate.

Since tryptophan is an amino acid found in protein, you might well ask why eating a protein-rich food such as meat or fish doesn't have the same effect. The reason is that tryptophan, in order to enter the brain, must compete with five other similarly shaped amino acids that all share the same system for being carried into the brain. The other amino acids in protein foods are more plentiful than tryptophan; tryptophan is the scarcest. So when you eat some eggs or fish or meat, there are more of these competing amino acids than tryptophan being digested and sent into the blood.

Therefore tryptophan has a much harder time getting into the brain. The result of eating a lot of protein is that the level of tryptophan in the brain does not increase and neither does the level of serotonin.

The way to increase the level of tryptophan in the brain is to eat starchy and sweet foods. When you eat carbohydrates, insulin is secreted into the blood, which at all times contains amino acids that are constantly moving between the blood and the cells. After insulin is secreted, these amino acids leave the blood very quickly and enter the muscle and other cells in the body. Tryptophan, however, is one amino acid that is not affected as much by insulin secretion. Tryptophan remains in the blood after the competition has disappeared. And with the competing amino acids out of the way, the tryptophan enters the brain easily, increases the amount of serotonin in the brain, and the serotonin sends out a signal that shuts off the carbohydrate hunger.

In other words, it takes carbohydrate foods to control carbohydrate hunger. But the carbohydrate food should be eaten alone, not with a food that contains protein or after a basically protein meal. For instance, eat crackers by themselves, not with cheese, and do not end a fish dinner with a handful of cookies. If protein is combined with carbohydrate, the other amino acids from the protein will be competing with the tryptophan to get into the brain. Much less tryptophan will enter the brain than if you had eaten carbohydrate by itself.

A weight-reducing plan currently being promoted suggests eating specific kinds of protein to increase brain tryptophan and avoiding other kinds, which may decrease brain tryptophan. The increase or decrease in the amount of tryptophan in your brain is supposed to make you happy or sad: If you are happy you will eat less and if you are sad you will eat more. The dietary recommendations are nonsense and the conclusion that you become happy or sad after eating certain foods has no scientific basis.

No protein will increase brain tryptophan; all protein foods contain so much more of the competing amino acids than tryptophan that the level of tryptophan in the brain will stay the same or even be lowered slightly. Eating carbohydrates is the only way to increase brain tryptophan. Furthermore, when brain tryptophan is increased, and along with it brain serotonin, the only emotions you will experience (and this information also comes from ongoing research at MIT) are relaxation and calmness. At MIT volunteers were given tryptophan and then a battery of psychological tests: Their feelings of happiness or sadness did not change after taking tryptophan or an inert placebo.

This research on the carbohydrate connection

between the diet and the brain stimulated our search for a specific carbohydrate hunger. We began some studies on rats in our laboratory. We assumed that if rats needed to eat carbohydrates, it wouldn't be because their mothers had given them cookies when they fell out of their cages or ice cream when their tails were pinched. We discovered that the rats did, indeed, have a specific hunger for carbohydrates, and when they were allowed to control the amount they ate, they ate a constant proportion every day. It didn't matter whether the carbohydrate was a sweet or a starch: They ate the same amount.

We also found that after their carbohydrate hunger was satisfied, the rats went on to eat something else. In one experiment we fed half our rats six calories' worth of sugary homemade mints and the other half six calories' worth of peanut butter, which is mostly fat. Then we gave both sets of rats a choice of two foods, one containing a lot of carbohydrate, the other very little. The mint-fed rats were obviously satisfied with the sugar in their candy because they chose to eat the low-carbohydrate food. The rats who had been fed peanut butter, on the other hand, ate primarily the high-carbohydrate food.

What this meant was not only that a carbohydrate hunger exists, but that when it is satisfied, it goes away. We learned that serotonin is involved in turning off this hunger by giving rats a drug that increased the activity of this brain chemical. The rats treated with the drug ate much less carbohydrate (but not protein) than rats given an inert placebo. It seemed to us that a cycle occurs when carbohydrates are eaten. The sweet or starchy food causes insulin to be secreted and in turn causes tryptophan to enter the brain easily and make serotonin. Serotonin then sends out a signal saying "Stop eating any more carbohydrate."

These results suggested the possibility of devising a diet that would satisfy the carbohydrate craver's need for carbohydrate. Such a diet would promote weight loss without causing an insatiable longing for sweet and starchy foods. It would be a low-calorie diet that contained enough carbohydrate at and between meals to cause serotonin to shut off the carbohydrate hunger. But first we wanted to make sure that a carbohydrate hunger really exists in people.

We next turned our attention to people, specifically overweight people who claimed to overeat only carbohydrate foods. You'll find a description of our research in the next chapter, in which I ask you to take your own carbohydrate-craving test. For now, it's enough to say that our human volunteers confirmed what we had already found out with our laboratory rats: People, too, have a distinct hunger for carbohydrates, and serotonin is involved in its regulation.

But if it is true, as our research showed, that people and rats have a need for carbohydrates, why can't the human carbohydrate craver be more like the rat, and satisfy the craving with only small amounts of carbohydrate?

The answer is twofold. The first is that humans trying to lose weight go on diets that deprive them of the carbohydrates the body needs. The second is that when carbohydrate cravers do eat carbohydrates, they feel guilty. Both these factors make people overeat.

When you go on a diet that eliminates all but the small amounts of carbohydrates found in fruit and vegetables, your body temporarily loses its ability to control its carbohydrate hunger. We found that when our rats were deprived of carbohydrates for a few weeks, they responded by binging, by eating much more carbohydrate than normal, because the signal from the brain that says "Stop, you've had enough" was not produced soon enough. The delay may occur because a smaller-than-usual amount of insulin is secreted when carbohydrates have not been eaten for several days. That's why you aren't satisfied with eating a small amount of carbohydrate after you go off one of those high-protein–low-carbohydrate diets. You, like the rats, have to eat a lot of carbohydrate to produce enough serotonin to shut off your carbohydrate hunger.

The other thing that happens is that your guilt and anxiety over eating these "fattening" foods prevent you from realizing that your carbohydrate hunger is finally satisfied. People who are able to control their carbohydrate hunger with normal amounts of carbohydrate are aware of feeling better after snacking or eating a high-carbohydrate meal.

A patient explained, "I always feel a little uptight and tense before my snack. I have difficulty concentrating on my work. Then I go and eat my cookies and afterward, what a change. I feel relaxed, I can focus on what I have to finish, and I no longer feel irritable."

How do you feel after you start eating carbohydrates again? Probably as relaxed as the boy caught with his hand in the cookie jar. You see yourself eating those cookies or ice cream and you feel guilty, angry, tense, upset, and, of course, totally oblivious to any sign that you have eaten enough. The signal to stop eating carbohydrate is there, but you ignore it. And you continue to eat carbohydrate long after your body's needs have been satisfied.

At this point, you may be thinking, "Yes, I have a problem with a carbohydrate hunger but why should I bother dieting? I might as well buy that stuff called starch blockers. According to the ads and books, I can gorge myself on crackers or cookies and never gain an ounce."

Sounds great, doesn't it? Unfortunately, it won't work. Your carbohydrate hunger will not be satisfied. Imagine yourself being very thirsty and drinking cup after cup of water, but because of some problem with your stomach, the water never gets into your body — it just pours out of you. Do you think your thirst would be slaked? No, you would just become frantic because you could never seem to satisfy it.

Starch blockers work in the following way. In order for carbohydrate to get from your intestinal tract into your bloodstream, it must be digested, that is, broken down into its simplest form, which is done by enzymes. The starch blocker prevents one of these carbohydrate-digesting enzymes from working. So after you eat crackers, or bread or cookies or candy, these foods simply sit around in your intestinal tract, probably being fermented a bit by the bacteria that live in your intestine and producing some gas because of the fermentation. Eventually, you eliminate all this undigested food.

Seems like the perfect solution to overeating carbohydrates, doesn't it? It's not, for two reasons:

First, your carbohydrate hunger will still be there. The only way it can be turned off is by eating and *digesting* carbohydrate so it enters your blood. And then, as you already know, insulin is released, the amino acid tryptophan enters the brain, more serotonin is made, and the carbohydrate hunger is shut off. The starch blockers prevent this first step, the digestion of carbohydrate, from occurring. The result is that you will stuff more and more carbohydrates into your body (just as you might drink more and more water if none got into your body) in the vain attempt to shut off the carbohydrate hunger. I hate to think of what your intestines might look like, carrying around several pounds of undigested cookies, pasta, and bread.

The second reason these starch blockers are not good is that no one has yet done any research on what else might be leaving your intestinal tract undigested along with the carbohydrates. It is entirely possible that valuable minerals — iron, zinc, or calcium, for example — which are not easily absorbed into the blood from the intestinal tract under the best of conditions, might be passing out along with all this undigested material. So you may be risking a mineral deficiency by taking starch blockers, especially for long periods of time. Supplements won't help because they are also taken by mouth and, like food, must be absorbed in the intestine.

The only way to control your carbohydrate hunger is to eat carbohydrates. It's simple, it's easy, and it works.

———————

The Carbohydrate Craver's Diet is based on hard scientific research, but it has been tested on living carbohydrate cravers. It works for them, and it will work for you, because it is the only diet that takes away your feeling of carbohydrate hunger and teaches you how to control it — not by depriving you of carbohydrates, as most other diets do — but by including them in your weight-loss program.

The Carbohydrate Craver's Diet makes sure you eat carbohydrates at every meal and, just as important, that you eat a carbohydrate-rich snack once a day, when your carbohydrate hunger is most intense. As long as your body is fed the carbohydrate it demands every day, the overeating that follows deprivation will be prevented. Your body will be able to regulate your carbohydrate hunger and make you feel satisfied with only moderate amounts.

You also will stop the overeating that is caused by guilt. How can you feel guilty about snacking on a candy bar or a jelly-coated muffin when you are eating only 1100 calories a day and losing weight? Because the diet allows you to snack every single day, you don't have to overeat one day because you are going to be deprived the next.

The diet also teaches you to "listen" for the signal that says that your carbohydrate hunger is satisfied. This means that, for the first time, you will be able to eat the carbohydrate you crave without overeating.

And since your carbohydrate hunger is always satisfied, and you lose your guilt along with those extra pounds, you will be able to stay on the diet for as long as you need to.

Another reason you can stay on this diet is that it is nutritionally complete. As a nutritionist, I could not in good conscience offer a diet that would undermine your nutritional health. Although it may not hurt you to subsist on a kooky diet for a couple of weeks, it surely would for a longer time. The reason the Carbohydrate Craver's Diet — which is as low in calories as most of the others — can still be nutritionally sound is that foods on the diet are very high in vitamins and minerals.

How much weight will you lose on the Carbohydrate Craver's Diet? Ten pounds or a hundred, depending on your goals and the length of time you stay on the diet. This is not a miracle quick-weight-loss diet. If there really were miracle diets, we wouldn't need a new miracle every year. And the statistics wouldn't show that 95 percent of the people who go on diets ultimately fail.

The Carbohydrate Craver's Diet is a *steady* weight-loss program. The weight you lose will be fat pounds, not just water loss. Carbohydrates hold water, so if you remove them from your diet, you'll quickly lose a few pounds in water. The minute you go back to eating carbohydrates, the water poundage will come back just as quickly, and so will the other pounds you'll gain from binging to overcome deprivation.

On 1100 calories a day, you should lose 1 or 2 pounds a week. (I'll talk more about this in Chapter 3.) The average person should lose a *minimum* of 10 pounds in two months, 25 pounds in six, and 50 pounds in a year. And you'll really be comfortable while doing it.

The Carbohydrate Craver's Diet offers you 900 calories a day in meals and 200 in snacks. You won't have to count the calories because we've done it for you. You'll find two versions of the diet, one for people who like to eat meat, chicken, and fish, and another for those who prefer to get their protein from grain and bean combinations, dairy products, and small amounts of chicken or fish. We have special diet plans for special needs and occasions; you'll learn more about all of these later.

Now it is time to establish your own carbohydrate-craving profile.

2

The
Carbohydrate-Craving
Test

"When do I need a snack? Why, between four and five, and nine and ten,
when it's carbohydrate-craving time."
— *Patient A*

"I'm a chain cracker eater. I eat carbohydrates all day long, so how can I tell
you when I crave them most?"
— *Patient B*

THE TEST you'll take in this chapter will give you
the answers to two simple but important questions:

1. Are you really a carbohydrate craver?

2. If you are one, when do your peak craving periods occur?

You need the answer to the first question because
the Carbohydrate Craver's Diet is not an all-pur-
pose diet for everyone; it is designed specifically to
enable people with carbohydrate cravings to lose

weight. You need the answer to the second question because calorie-controlled snacking is basic to the Carbohydrate Craver's Diet. Snacking is what makes it possible for you not only to lose weight, but to lose it in a satisfying way, so that you'll be able to stick to the diet for as long as you need to.

Many carbohydrate cravers are aware of their hunger for these foods and also aware of the time of day their cravings occur. If you are sure that you are a carbohydrate craver — as distinct from someone who is chronically hungry because of skipped or too-skimpy meals, or a nibbler who always has to have something going from hand to mouth — and if you also know what time your peak craving periods occur each day, you don't need to take this test. But read the chapter anyway to be sure you haven't misinterpreted your hunger.

Basically, this diagnostic test is a very simple three-day version of the experiments we ran with volunteers at MIT. All you need is a pencil and a small notebook and a supply of two kinds of snacks. I'll give you directions in a moment, but first let me tell you a little bit about our laboratory experiment.

———————

When we were ready to shift our focus from rats to people, we decided to choose not just any people but overweight people who claimed they overate *only* starchy and sweet foods. These carbohydrate cravers were of particular interest to us because of the argument against carbohydrate hunger put forth by a Yale research psychologist.

"Of course obese people eat sweet and starchy foods," she said. "They overeat anything available, and carbohydrate foods are more available than meat or cheese or fish sticks."

To test this argument, we made sure that our volunteers had easy and equal access to both protein and carbohydrate foods. The foods had the same caloric values, and we tried to make both types of food tasty and attractive. For the protein, we chose meat and cheese snacks of the cocktail appetizer type. The carbohydrates included both starchy and sweet foods.

Our twenty-four volunteers lived in an MIT dormitory, where they were fed meals containing 1000 calories a day. In addition, they were permitted to eat as many snacks as they liked. The only restriction was that they had to select all their snacks from our refrigerated vending machine, which contained five protein snacks and five carbohydrate snacks. To get the food, the volunteer entered a code into the computer attached to the machine. The computer recorded the name of the person who took the snack, the name of the snack, and the time the snack was taken. At the end of our first two weeks, we had a record of when and what each person ate for a snack.

Our findings confirmed what our subjects had told us — that indeed they did overeat only carbohydrate foods — and disproved the psychologist's theory that overweight people will eat anything, so long as it is available. Twenty-three of our volunteers chose an average of four carbohydrate snacks a day and only one protein snack. Furthermore, the record showed that each tended to snack at the same time each day according to a personal carbohydrate-craving clock. Even more interesting, we found that each of our volunteers ate just about the same number of snacks a day, regardless of their schedule of activities or of circumstances that one would suppose would increase or decrease their snacking. Our laboratory rats also had shown a tendency to eat the same amount of carbohydrate every day.

Our next step was to see if the carbohydrate hunger demonstrated by our human volunteers was controlled by brain serotonin, as it was in our rats. With their permission, some of our subjects took small doses of a safe drug that increases the activity of brain serotonin. Others took an inert substance; neither subjects nor the researchers knew who had taken the drug and who the placebo.

At the end of two more weeks, we found that the

volunteers on the placebo had continued to eat the same number of snacks as they did before. Those who received the experimental drug ate considerably fewer carbohydrate snacks.

These results convinced us that carbohydrate hunger in humans is real and under the control of this brain neurotransmitter, serotonin. Serotonin apparently is involved in shutting off the sensation of a carbohydrate hunger because when it becomes more active through the use of drugs, animals and people eat less carbohydrate.

I realized that there was a very simple way to make serotonin shut off carbohydrate hunger so that people who always ate too much would finally be able to control the amount of carbohydrate they ate. This was to make sure that when a person felt a hunger for carbohydrate, that person ate carbohydrate. Eating carbohydrate would cause more serotonin to be made, and serotonin would send out the signal to stop eating any more carbohydrate. Most people didn't need drugs; they simply had to know when their carbohydrate hunger was most intense, and they had to eat some carbohydrate at that time. It became obvious why high-protein–low-carbohydrate diets fail — these diets do not cause enough serotonin to be produced to shut off the carbohydrate hunger.

With this knowledge, it was possible to create a weight-loss diet that will work for carbohydrate

cravers. This diet would provide enough carbohydrate at meals and also at that time of day when the
carbohydrate craving is strongest, to satisfy the carbohydrate hunger and activate the serotonin shut-
off switch.

The diet, of course, would have to be low in calories. (Don't believe any claims for diets that say
calories don't count; people usually lose weight because they become so sick of the food that they eat
less or they actually become sick.) But it was not
difficult to devise a low-calorie–high-carbohydrate
diet because, as our research showed, it took a *relatively small amount of carbohydrate-rich foods,
eaten at certain very specific times,* to satisfy the
carbohydrate craving. Furthermore, since many
starchy carbohydrates, like grains and beans, are
high in nutrients, the dieter could have his carbohydrates and vitamins and minerals too. Best of all
for the dieter, we could devise a diet that would
satisfy the carbohydrate craver's hunger.

I have tested the Carbohydrate Craver's Diet
with my own patients, many of whom came to me
because nothing else (including stapling the stomach) had ever worked. This diet works.

Now it's time to run your own experiment to deter-
mine your carbohydrate-craving profile. Look at

the list of carbohydrate snacks and the list of protein (or nibbling) snacks on page 23. I want you to select *one* snack from each group. Choose a snack that you like, but not one that you are passionately addicted to, that you would eat whether or not you felt like eating *something*, for that will affect the research results.

In the same way, try to choose an acceptable commercial product, but not the best one ever. For example, you should snack on packaged brownies, not bakery ones — or, heaven forbid, delicious homemade ones. This is a research experiment, not a gourmet eating experience.

If possible, simply for convenience, buy packages in the required size. But if you can't find, say, a 1-ounce package of nuts, buy a pound and divide the nuts into sixteen portions; place them in plastic bags sealed with a tie. Try to make up enough snack packages, both of the carbohydrate and the nibbling varieties, to last through the whole experiment. If you have any left over at the end, give them away or save the carbohydrate snacks for the diet.

You'll need a pretty good supply of the two snacks, enough to last you for three days (although, of course, you can go out and replenish your stock). If you leave the house in the morning and stay away all day, you should probably carry six of each of the two types of snacks with you.

The Carbohydrate-Craving Test Snacks

Carbohydrate Snacks

Any 1-ounce candy bar without nuts
1 package Pepperidge Farm Snack Bar
2 1-ounce packages Sun-Maid dried fruit
1 ounce of potato chips, corn chips, or
  pretzels
1 packaged brownie
1 muffin

Nibbling Snacks

1-ounce package of any kind of nuts
1-ounce package pumpkin or sunflower
  seeds
1-ounce package trail mix (nut and dried
  fruit combination)
1-ounce package bacon or pork rinds
2-ounce wedge of processed cheese
4 saltines with 1 ounce of any cheese

During the three-day test period, you must eat three meals a day, even if you are normally accustomed to skipping breakfast. If you miss a meal, it will be impossible to tell whether you are snacking because you are hungry for carbohydrates, or because you're just plain hungry, or because you are a chronic nibbler. Similarly, you should not try to keep to a diet during the three-day test, especially not a high-protein–low-carbohydrate diet, which starves your body for carbohydrates.

Along with your snacks, carry a small notebook and a pencil. Every time you eat a snack, enter the time of day in the notebook and put next to it a *C* if you ate a carbohydrate snack and an *N* if you ate a nibbling snack.

During the test period, you are not to eat any other snack but the ones you selected from the list. Every time you feel the urge to eat, ask yourself whether you are feeling a need to eat carbohydrates or just to put something in your mouth — and choose your snack accordingly. But choose it. And eat it right away. If you tell yourself, "I really want those cookies (or that piece of cheese) but I know I shouldn't," you will defeat the purpose of the test.

Eat your snack and record it before you eat another one. If you think you may be tempted to binge and eat them all up at once, you can prevent such binging by forcing yourself to take at least five minutes to eat your snack.

The only time you should try *not* to snack, even if you feel like it, is thirty minutes before a meal. Your desire for something to eat at that time really may be related to simple hunger.

If something comes up to disrupt your schedule during the three-day test period, simply skip that day and add an extra day to the test. It's best not to test yourself on days that are stressful or unpredictable. And definitely don't take the test just before your menstrual period, since women typically have an increased need for sweets at that time. Later, you will learn how to take care of that by following my Premenstrual Sweet Tooth suggestions, but for now, while you are trying to find out your normal carbohydrate-craving cycle, you want to avoid anything that may give you an unusual pattern.

One factor that can interfere with, or at least inhibit, your research is the presence of other people. After all, what will your co-workers (who know you are always on one diet or another) think when they see you actually munching away at a cookie? If you don't want to go into long explanations, you can always say you are taking a test to "monitor my daily rhythm of carbohydrate ingestion." This sounds medical enough so that most people will have the decency not to pursue it further. Anyway, it's true.

At the end of the three days, it's time to see what your research shows. We'll analyze it first for carbohydrate cravings (if any) and second for your pattern of nibbling (if you show one). One sheet of lined paper is all you'll need. Down the left-hand side of the sheet, mark the hours of the day and indicate your usual mealtimes. The paper will look like the one on page 27.

Now go to your little notebook and transfer each of the Cs you have recorded — for all of the days — to the line on your tally sheet next to the hour during which you ate the carbohydrate snack. The illustration on page 28 is an example of what a typical chart might look like.

The time period in which the Cs cluster most densely is your carbohydrate-craving time. When you start your diet, that hour will be your snack time. If your Cs appear in two clusters, you may need to snack twice a day; the diet has provisions for this too.

If, in addition to the one or two obvious craving periods, you find that you snacked at least twice each day, at other times, you may need to eat more carbohydrate at your meals in addition to eating carbohydrate as snacks. Your choice of diet, in this case, should be the Carbohydrate Dense Diet, since that offers more carbohydrates at mealtimes than does the Carbohydrate Craver's Basic Diet. I'll explain more about that in Chapters 7 and 8, the diet chapters; just keep it in mind for now.

Now look at your chart to see if you routinely ended a meal with a dessert snack — or if you

Three-Day
Carbohydrate-Snack Record

7:00 A.M. _____

8:00 (breakfast) _____

9:00 _____

10:00 _____

11:00 _____

12:00 (lunch) _____

1:00 P.M. _____

2:00 _____

3:00 _____

4:00 _____

5:00 _____

6:00 (dinner) _____

7:00 _____

8:00 _____

9:00 _____

10:00 _____

11:00 (bed) _____

Three-Day
Carbohydrate-Snack Record

7:00 A.M.	
8:00 (breakfast)	
9:00	
10:00	
11:00	*C*
12:00 (lunch)	
1:00 P.M.	
2:00	
3:00	*C C C*
4:00	*C C C C*
5:00	*C C*
6:00	
7:00 (dinner)	
8:00	
9:00	
10:00	*C*
11:00 (bed)	

snacked shortly after a meal. If you did, that probably means you have trouble finishing a meal without something sweet. Since it is best not to eat your
carbohydrate snacks within an hour after finishing a
meal (because it takes longer to turn off carbohydrate hunger after you've eaten protein), once you
start the diet you might consider ending a meal
with a few sweet calories to make you feel satisfied.
A cup of coffee or tea with 2 teaspoons of sugar (32
calories) or a hard candy (about 20 calories) will satisfy your dessert sweet tooth without destroying
your diet.

Now, once again, look at your carbohydrate-
craving profile to see whether you regularly
snacked late at night. If that represents your peak
period, you are probably one of those people who
need carbohydrates before going to sleep. But if
you snacked at night in addition to one or two peak
periods during the day, you should try to analyze
why you need to eat at that hour.

Some people eat late at night to keep themselves
awake or to give themselves the energy they think
they need to finish a particular task. In that case,
however, carbohydrates are absolutely the wrong
foods to eat. As you already know, eating carbohydrates increases the manufacture of serotonin. And
serotonin (besides controlling further carbohydrate
consumption) makes the body feel sleepy. Fortunately, it does this most effectively at the time we

Three-Day
Nibbling-Snack Record

Time	
7:00 A.M.	
8:00 (breakfast)	
9:00	
10:00	N
11:00	
12:00 (lunch)	
1:00 P.M.	
2:00	
3:00	
4:00	
5:00	
6:00	N N
7:00 (dinner)	
8:00	N N N N
9:00	N N N N
10:00	N
11:00 (bed)	N

should be sleeping, otherwise we'd all doze off after our morning doughnut.

A patient once told me that she ate an entire can of cranberry sauce to keep herself awake long enough to finish a report. She fell asleep at the kitchen table. If you must stay awake and you need to eat, try an egg or cheese or a steak. These foods don't contain any carbohydrates. On the other hand, if you need to fall asleep, carbohydrates will help you do it.

———

When you finish analyzing your carbohydrate snacking pattern, do the same for your nibbling snacks. Transfer the *N*s to the same chart and, again, look to see where those snacks were clustered. A typical nibbler's chart, with nibbling snacks clustered during times when the patient was home and relaxing, appears on page 30.

With your chart in front of you, try to figure out why you do this type of eating at the times you do. Are you tired? Bored? Stressed? Lonely? Angry? Frustrated? Worried? Are you nibbling in order to take a break in your work? Do you nibble to delay starting a task you dislike doing? Do you eat when you are in the car, talking on the telephone, making a meal, relaxing with a book, or watching television? Simply by identifying the time of day when you are most likely to nibble, and by understanding some of the reasons why you do, you may be able to cut out some of this kind of eating. (Chapter 11 contains some hints for avoiding nibbling, and gives some suggestions for low-calorie nibbles if you can't stop completely.)

———————

The answers you obtained from taking the Carbohydrate-Craving Test have established your carbohydrate-eating profile. With this information, you are now ready to tackle the specifics of the Carbohydrate Craver's Diet.

3

How to Be a Loser

I'D LIKE TO BE ABLE to tell you that you are going to lose 25 pounds in two weeks on the Carbohydrate Craver's Diet, but if you did, you'd gain them all back. The quick-weight-loss diets are the ones that you, and millions like you, have been going on and falling off for years. Generally speaking, those are the diets you should stay on for only two weeks (if that) because they are usually so unbalanced as to be, at best, mildly unhealthy and, at worst, dangerously so. But above all the reason the quick-weight-loss diets don't work for you is that they cut out the food your body craves — carbohydrates.

We are people who want instant gratification. Fifteen pounds in two weeks sounds terrific. (Some diets promise you'll lose them in less.) But are those real pounds? By now, most of you who have sampled these diets are aware that the weight you lose quickly is water weight. Carbohydrates hold water; cut them out of your diet and you lose water pounds — until your body rebels and your carbohydrate cravings set you off on a binge of eating sweets and starches. Back come the pounds you starved yourself to lose.

How much real weight — fat weight, not water weight — will you lose on the Carbohydrate Craver's Diet? In the beginning, your rate of weight loss will depend on how many calories you were eating before you began the diet. If you were eating as few as 1600 calories a day (and I doubt that you were eating so few), your caloric intake would be reduced by 500 calories a day. At that rate you should lose 1 pound the first week. If, however, you were eating 3000 calories a day (1000 in meals and 2000 in cookies), your daily caloric intake would be decreased by 1900 calories. In this case, you should lose approximately 9 pounds in the first two weeks.

After that, the amount of weight you lose will usually settle down to 1 or 2 pounds a week — considered by medical authorities to be optimal for the final success of a diet — because your body is no longer responding to the initial large decrease in calories. As you know, you always lose weight rapidly when you start a diet. Then, during the remainder of the diet, you lose weight more slowly. On a fourteen-day crash program like the Scarsdale Diet, you've finished the diet before the slowdown occurs. The other reason you "lose" so much weight on crash diets is that they contain very little carbohydrate, and once carbohydrate is dropped from your diet, a lot of water is lost from the body. Of course, for the carbohydrate craver, these diets are simply impossible.

So, to recapitulate, the amount of weight you can expect to lose during the first two weeks of the diet will depend on how many calories you are eating now. My guess is that if you are a carbohydrate craver (and you are if you are reading this book) you consume many more calories a day than you think you do. A woman who took part in our vending machine study insisted that she gained weight if she ate more than 500 calories a day. She complained constantly that she was going to gain weight from our meals (they provided 1000 calories). Actually, she *did* gain weight on the study, but not from meals. According to her computer records, she was eating 3000 calories' worth of cookies every day.

Unless you have a robot recording the number of snacks you eat every day, you probably really don't know how many calories you consume. So you may be pleasantly surprised by your initial weight loss. The important thing, though, is to think of your weight loss in future terms. At the very slow loss rate of 1 pound a week, you will be 25 pounds thinner in six months.

How many pounds you decide to lose depends on two things: what you should weigh to be healthy and what you should weigh to believe that you look good. The first is easy. Most doctors agree that you should not weigh more than 10 to 15 percent above the weights given in standard height-weight charts. One such table appears on pages 38–39. Whether this weight will satisfy you depends on your own image of your ideal shape. Some people feel happy only if they look as though they had been shipwrecked without food for thirty days, and others are happy if they can finally see their toes.

Realistically, you should not go below the weights on the chart (there are medical risks in being too thin), and you should be content with a weight that is easy to maintain after the diet is over. Your body usually decides for you. Your weight loss slows down, and you seem to settle into a size that feels right and is most compatible with the eating and exercise you do after you stop dieting.

Stay on the diet as long as you have the determination to do so. Set small, easily reached goals, such as losing 10 pounds in two months. After that goal is reached, decide whether you want to continue or to stop for a while and maintain your weight loss. There is no rule engraved on a stone doughnut somewhere that says you must diet continuously. As long as you don't gain any weight during this rest period, you can stop the diet for as long as you want to.

Don't weigh yourself more than once a week. Less is better. Frequent weighings often give false readings, since a loss of half a pound, for example, can be offset by the amount of water you drank the night before or whether you are still digesting the cabbage you ate two dinners ago.

A better way of monitoring your weight loss is the zipper test. Select an article of clothing that is too tight at the start of the diet. Once a week, try to zip it up. As the weight comes off, the zipper will come up. When the zipper moves easily, try on something smaller and continue the test.

Diet-proof your kitchen before you start on the Carbohydrate Craver's Diet. Get rid of temptations; if your family will be snacking on food you also would like to eat, ask them to keep it elsewhere. If their snacks include ice cream and other foods that have to be kept in the refrigerator, this may be easier said than done. Perhaps an unmarked container covered with brown wrapping paper could be used? However, if you sit down and explain the diet to them, particularly the snack requirements (and restrictions), they are likely to be cooperative. Chapter 14 has more suggestions on avoiding the snacks of others.

Clear off a place on the kitchen counter for a food scale, measuring cups, and spoons. You need to

Desirable Weights

Men of Ages 25 and Over
Weight in pounds according to frame
(in indoor clothing)

HEIGHT with shoes on— 1-inch heels		SMALL FRAME	MEDIUM FRAME	LARGE FRAME
FEET	INCHES			
5	2	112–120	118–129	126–141
5	3	115–123	121–133	129–144
5	4	118–126	124–136	132–148
5	5	121–129	127–139	135–152
5	6	124–133	130–143	138–156
5	7	128–137	134–147	142–161
5	8	132–141	138–152	147–166
5	9	136–145	142–156	151–170
5	10	140–150	146–160	155–174
5	11	144–154	150–165	159–179
6	0	148–158	154–170	164–184
6	1	152–162	158–175	168–189
6	2	156–167	162–180	173–194
6	3	160–171	167–185	178–199
6	4	164–175	172–190	182–204

METROPOLITAN LIFE INSURANCE DATA

Desirable Weights

Women of Ages 25 and Over
Weight in pounds according to frame
(in indoor clothing)

HEIGHT *with shoes on– 2-inch heels* FEET	INCHES	SMALL FRAME	MEDIUM FRAME	LARGE FRAME
4	10	92–98	96–107	104–119
4	11	94–101	98–110	106–122
5	0	96–104	101–113	109–125
5	1	99–107	104–116	112–128
5	2	102–110	107–119	115–131
5	3	105–113	110–122	118–134
5	4	108–116	113–126	121–138
5	5	111–119	116–130	125–142
5	6	114–123	120–135	129–146
5	7	118–127	124–139	133–150
5	8	122–131	128–143	137–154
5	9	126–135	132–147	141–158
5	10	130–140	136–151	145–163
5	11	134–144	140–155	149–168
6	0	138–148	144–159	153–173

For girls between 18 and 25, subtract 1 pound for each year under 25. (Courtesy of Metropolitan Life Insurance Co.)

weigh and measure your food for the first three weeks of the diet. If your equipment is handy, you are more likely to do it.

Finally, don't start on the diet unless you are sure you want to lose weight NOW. If you see stress ahead, or any other situation that may make you overeat (like an unwanted relative moving in for the next month), wait. Diets, even satisfying ones like this, are somewhat stressful, and you are apt to be more successful if the rest of your life is relatively placid. But note the word *relative*. If you wait until life is totally placid, you will never begin.

4

The Carbohydrate Craver's Meal Plans

THERE ARE TWO Carbohydrate Craver's Diets. Superficially they may seem almost the same, and although they do have many of the same features, there are subtle but important differences between the two.

Both the Carbohydrate Craver's Basic Diet and the Carbohydrate Dense Diet provide 900 calories in meals and 200 calories in snacks. The caloric content of the meals is the same on both diet plans — breakfast, 200; lunch, 300; and dinner, 400.

Both diets provide essential nutrients that are often absent or inadequate in other weight-loss programs. Both provide enough carbohydrate to satisfy your cravings. For these reasons, you can select one diet or the other, and you can mix them up or alternate between them in any way. You'll always get your required nutrients and the right number of calories.

The Carbohydrate Craver's Basic Diet and the Carbohydrate Dense Diet differ in the following ways: Although both diets include carbohydrate-rich foods such as bread, potatoes, rice, and pasta, the Dense Diet offers larger portions of these foods than does the Basic Diet. In exchange, it offers slightly smaller portions of protein foods like meat. Furthermore, the protein in the Dense Diet is partially provided by combining carbohydrate foods and by protein-fortified pastas.

You should probably go on the Carbohydrate Dense Diet, at least in the beginning, if your carbohydrate-craving profile showed that you need carbohydrate foods throughout the day, rather than at one peak craving period.

If you tend to prefer vegetables and starchy foods to meat and fish, the menus on the Dense Diet will appeal to you also.

Protein in the Carbohydrate Craver's Basic Diet is supplied in the more traditional way, through meat, fish, and poultry. Since you don't have to spend quite so much time in preparing these foods as you do in cooking grains and pasta, the Basic Diet is a good choice for the person who likes quick meals — and whose craving profile showed the need to eat carbohydrate snacks only at one or two peak craving periods. On the Basic Diet, you'll find some very fast meals that involve no cooking at all.

You are free to switch from one diet to the other for particular meals if you realize that your carbohydrate hunger at meals varies throughout the day. You may be the sort of person who is happy with very little carbohydrate at breakfast and lunch but unsatisfied without a lot of carbohydrate at dinner. Or you may need to eat carbohydrate at breakfast and lunch and prefer to dig into a piece of meat for dinner.

If you start on the Dense Diet, you may find that after a few weeks of having your carbohydrate hunger always satisfied, your need for carbohydrate is decreasing slightly. Experiment with some meals from the Basic Diet to see if this is the case. Since the menus require less time to prepare, knowing that you can feel carbohydrate "full" on those meals will be useful when you don't have much time for meal preparation.

There will be days when you wake up absolutely aching to eat carbohydrates and other days when even you, the carbohydrate craver, will have fantasies about a juicy steak. Such is the nature of our bodies. On those days, find menus that appeal to you the most from each of the diet plans.

When you start dieting, however, I think you should make your life as simple as possible. Pick whichever diet seems best for your needs and plan your first week's menus. You can follow the menus in any order, and you may find it easier to eat the same one or two breakfasts and lunches every day for a week. This will cut down on both your shopping and preparation time.

For dinner, you'll find that some of the menus are grouped together so that food prepared for one meal can be used in meals on the following days. Chicken can last for three meals, and rice cooked for dinner one night can make a lunch salad the next day.

To succeed on either of the Carbohydrate Craver's Diets, you must eat your daily snack — I'll discuss that in detail in Chapter 5 — and you must eat three meals a day. You must not skip a meal because you will overeat at your next meal (or not be able to stop with one snack if your snack time follows the skipped meal). But just because you have to eat three meals a day, that doesn't mean you have to eat them at traditional mealtimes. Here are some suggestions to help you succeed in following the Carbohydrate Craver's Diets.

Breakfast

If you find eating breakfast difficult because you aren't hungry early in the morning or have very little time, then delay eating this meal until later in the morning. Take breakfast with you and have it when you arrive at work. If you are at home, wait until you have been up for an hour, and then eat. If your snack time occurs during the morning, make sure that it doesn't coincide with a delayed breakfast; wait an hour after the meal is over before eating the snack.

———

I know someone who always does her cooking early in the morning because she is never tempted to nibble. She can even make cookies for her son's class or other temptations like birthday cakes because the thought of eating causes her to become slightly nauseated. Consider doing your cooking then if you have the same response.

Lunch

Don't skip lunch or eat less than the recommended amounts.

If you do, you may find yourself extremely hungry late in the afternoon. Should that also be your snack time, you won't find your stomach satisfied with the snack even if your carbohydrate craving is.

———

If you eat lunch away from home, use a wide-mouth Thermos bottle and plastic bags with zip-locked enclosures for sandwiches and salads. Keep a few cans of water-packed tuna fish, a can opener, and a plastic fork in a desk drawer for times when you forget to carry your lunch from home. If there is a local salad bar handy, buy some green pepper, carrots, and cabbage, add the tuna, and eat one slice of bread, without butter.

Dinner

Dinner is sometimes only the first course in an evening of eating. If you tend to nibble away your evenings, time the start of dinner to minimize the time between eating and going to bed. Plan activities for the early part of the evening, like going to an exercise class, walking the dog, late shopping, phone calls, returning books to the library, watching the evening news, or doing the laundry. Start dinner around eight, and eat very slowly. Drink one or two cups of tea, coffee, or a no-caffeine beverage after the meal is over. By starting late and stretching the time, you won't have much opportunity to eat later on.

Finishing the meal is also difficult, especially if you sit around the table to talk. If there is food on the table, you will find yourself picking at it, even if you aren't hungry. Prevent eating by clearing the table and serving a hot beverage to talk over; if you sweeten yours with one or two teaspoons of sugar you will be satisfied even if others are having some dessert.

If you are a "kitchen picker" who must nibble while cleaning up, prevent picking by sucking on a hard candy. If your mouth is filled with the taste of something sweet, you won't be tempted to nibble on leftovers. Or you can do what a friend of mine has learned to do.

"I know it sounds crazy," she says, "but I enjoy dinner only when I can have it alone in the kitchen. No matter what I eat at the table, I still want something while I'm washing the dishes. So I've learned to measure out my food and save it for after the rest of the family has eaten."

Leftovers are hazardous to your diet. Unless you are going to use some for another diet meal, put them where they won't tempt you, like in the freezer compartment of the refrigerator.

––––––

If you don't have a dog who can conveniently eat your leftovers, train your neighborhood birds. I had a neighbor who fed a clan of crows every evening with her leftovers. They ate absolutely everything, with the exception of raw onions.

––––––

Delaying after-dinner clean-up for an hour or so will diminish your nibbling also. Engage in a non-food activity after dinner, such as returning a phone call, helping a child with homework, or paying bills. Or, if you must clean up immediately, do it as fast as possible and plan something pleasurable after you leave the kitchen, like a favorite TV show or reading a good book or going to the movies.

Weekends can lead to haphazard eating. Avoid skipping meals by being flexible about when you eat them. Eat breakfast whenever you feel like it, lunch four or five hours later (even though it may be midafternoon), and dinner late in the evening. If you sleep until noon or later, eat lunch and dinner at their regular hours and eat breakfast before you go to bed.

If you are used to eating large quantities of food, you may be hungry during the first two or three days of the diet. If the hunger persists after three or four days, try the following:

1. Fill up on very-low-calorie bulky foods like cucumbers, sauerkraut, bean sprouts, alfalfa sprouts, and dill pickles.

2. Drink diet soda.

3. Add 100 calories of fat to your meals. Fat delays the emptying of the stomach and makes you feel full longer. Add 1 tablespoon of butter, sour cream, cream cheese, peanut butter, or cream to your least filling meals. Although this slight increase in calories will delay slightly the time it takes to reach your weight goal, it is worth doing if it makes the difference between being comfortable on the diet or unhappy.

If you are in the habit of taking a daily vitamin or mineral supplement, of course you can continue to do so, but the diet, unlike most weight-loss programs, doesn't require it, since all your nutritional needs are met in the foods. The only exception may be iron, which is generally deficient in the average American diet. If you don't eat much meat or shellfish, either eat an iron-fortified breakfast cereal or take a supplement.

Vitamins A and C and folic acid are richly supplied in the daily Super Salad, which you are required to eat on both diets. As long as you have your salad, you can pick and choose among the other vegetables on the exchange lists without concern for meeting your needs for these essential vitamins. The Super Salad takes care of them.

You'll also find milk and dairy products on each day's menu, which ensure you an adequate calcium supply. Calcium is a nutrient that people on diets are likely to skimp on, either because they forget to eat dairy foods or, more likely, because they think of them as fattening. Since a lifelong failure to eat enough calcium can lead to a bone disease called osteoporosis (especially in women), this important mineral is in plentiful supply on the Carbohydrate Craver's Diet plans.

However, you won't find alcohol in any amount on the diets because it is impossible to allow calories for alcoholic beverages and snacks without exceeding the 1100-calorie limit. Since you are a craver of carbohydrates in edible forms, the snacks are essential — the alcohol is not. Moreover, alcohol, with the exception of beer, contains very little carbohydrate. And you would have to drink several cans of beer to satisfy your carbohydrate needs — at the cost of several hundred unwanted calories.

5

The Snacks

> "Everyone at work knows that I have
> been on every conceivable diet, and
> never lost an ounce. So when I pulled
> out my bag of candy and started eating
> it during the afternoon break, they all
> looked at me as if I was crazy."
> — *A patient*

SNACKS ARE at the very heart of the Carbohydrate Craver's Diet. They are not a gimmick, and they are not a 200-calorie reward for good dieting behavior. They are fundamental to the diet. A carbohydrate-rich snack, eaten at your peak craving period, is what makes the diet work. It's also what enables you to stay with the diet for as long as you need to.

So forget what your mother told you about not eating between meals; forget what the other diets say about the immorality of cookies. Ignore your co-workers, or explain why you are eating the candy. You *must* snack every day on the Carbohydrate Craver's Diet.

You'll find a list of snacks on pages 62–73, with the portion size, the amount of carbohydrate, and the total calories in each. The starchy and sweet snacks are listed in order of their carbohydrate content, starting with those that have the highest amount of carbohydrate. In order to activate the carbohydrate-serotonin connection, you must eat a food that has a minimum of 25 grams of carbohydrate because it takes at least 25 grams of carbohydrate to release a sufficient amount of insulin to get tryptophan into the brain. In order to keep to your daily caloric limit, those 25 grams of carbohydrate must be contained in a snack that has no more than 200 calories. If your test analysis showed that you need two snacks a day, choose snacks with 170 or fewer calories, but be sure that there is a minimum of 25 grams of carbohydrate in each snack. Two-a-day snackers do not have to deduct the extra calories from their meals.

When you look through the snack list, you'll notice that certain snacks are considerably higher in carbohydrate than others, ranging from about 25 to over 60 grams. Certainly in the beginning, at least, I would suggest that you choose a higher-carbohydrate snack.

I'm going to ask you to eat the same snack every day for two weeks. After that, you can switch to another snack for the next two weeks. If you tempt yourself with an endless variety of snacks, you'll be eating to satisfy your taste buds, not your carbohydrate hunger — and it will be much more difficult to control your snacking. For the same reasons, don't choose a snack to which you are addicted. Buy prepackaged snacks wherever possible. The size will be more consistent — in a bakery, you are likely to point to the biggest cookie on the shelf — and if the commercially packaged snack isn't quite as delicious as the bakery one, all the better. Please don't cook your own snacks. I know some diet programs have you spend endless time preparing food. My philosophy is just the opposite — keep out of the kitchen as much as you can — and I certainly don't want you to hang around the oven baking cookies!

The high-carbohydrate foods on the snack list are of three general types — sweets, starches, and fruits. It makes no difference whether you choose a sweet or a starchy snack; it's a matter of taste. If you eat a sweet, sticky snack, though, try to brush your teeth afterward so you don't gain cavities while you lose pounds.

Although fruits are a high-carbohydrate food, they may not be quite as carbohydrate-satisfying as the other snacks. The carbohydrate in fruit is fructose. Less insulin is released after fructose is eaten than after sucrose or starches are eaten. Since the changes in the blood and brain that cause the carbohydrate hunger to be turned off depend on a certain amount of insulin being released, you may have to eat more fruit than you would other carbohydrate foods to bring about these changes.

If you want to make fruit your daily snack, but aren't sure whether it will satisfy your carbohydrate craving, try combining it with a dense carbohydrate snack like crackers or popcorn. Just don't go over your 200-calorie limit.

On the Carbohydrate Craver's Diet there is no such thing as a "good" snack or a "bad" snack. There are only high-carbohydrate snacks and low-carbohydrate snacks. From that standpoint, a piece of candy may be a better snack than a vitamin-filled orange. The snacks are not needed to fill your vitamin and mineral needs — the meals do that — but only to supply you with the pleasure and satisfaction that eating carbohydrate brings. So don't turn down a snack just because you've always felt guilty about eating it; this diet should help you lose your guilt along with your extra pounds.

Certain foods, although they may be rich in carbohydrates, do not appear on the snack table because they are, alas, also rich in fat — and therefore far too caloric. To get your minimum of 25 grams of carbohydrate, you'd have to eat a lot more than 200 calories. As you may suspect, these high-fat foods include pies (the pastry is full of shortening), some chocolate products (cocoa butter is all fat), ice cream (high in butter fat), and frosted or custard-filled pastries.

Some other foods aren't on the snack list because they come packaged in the wrong size — one item doesn't give you enough carbohydrate; two give you too many calories. Many candy bars fall into this category. Not many people, and certainly very few carbohydrate cravers, have the will power to throw away or save one quarter of a Snickers bar to stay within the 200-calorie limit.

Sizes of commercial snack products change frequently, so please check the size of a food against those given in the snack list at the end of this chapter. If it is different and you can figure out the amount of carbohydrate and the number of calories for the new size, fine. If not, choose a different snack.

There is nothing complicated about snacking on the Carbohydrate Craver's Diet. Basically, all you need to do is select a snack from the list and eat it at the time of day your test showed to be your peak craving period. That's all there is to it. Except that for a chronic failed dieter — and so many carbohydrate cravers are just that — it's awfully hard to get used to thinking that yesterday's dietary evil is now an integral and necessary part of your diet. Here are some hints that should help you snack successfully.

The Appropriate Snack

Although I've said that there is no such thing as a good or a bad snack, *in general,* there is a bad snack for you as an individual. That is the snack food to which you are addicted. This is no time to prove what stern stuff you are made of; unless you are de- termined to fail, don't select a snack food that you absolutely can't resist. Don't be like a friend of mine who thought she could control her addiction to chocolate chips by weighing and wrapping them in 1¼-ounce packages and storing them so she could eat one package a day. It took her fifteen minutes to wrap them up and another fifteen min- utes to tear them open and eat every last one.

Going Public

After a lifetime of eating like a bird when other people were around and (let's face it) like a pig in the privacy of your own car or closet, it's not going to be easy for you to come right out and snack in public. Yet because your test probably showed your peak craving periods occurring when others are around, you will have to learn how to snack in public.

The patient quoted at the beginning of this chap- ter met the challenge head-on. When one of her co-workers asked what in the world she was doing ("I thought you were on a diet, Janet!"), she replied, "I am. This snack is part of the diet."

By the time she had finished explaining the principle of the Carbohydrate Craver's Diet to them — and added that she had already started losing weight — they were intrigued instead of critical. And Janet had finished her gumdrops.

You may find your own habit of secret snacking harder to break, but you *must* break it in order to succeed on the diet. When you eat secretly, you eat too fast and you tend to eat much more carbohydrate than your body needs. You are also usually so anxious about being discovered, or so mad at yourself for what you are doing, that you rarely notice the feelings of contentment and relaxation that accompany eating carbohydrate.

But remember, that was the past. Now you are supposed to be snacking — you *have* to eat that snack. And you have to eat it *slowly*.

The Inconvenient Craving Time

If your peak carbohydrate-craving period occurs when you are regularly involved in a staff meeting at work, you are obviously going to have to adjust your snack time. (Even I wouldn't suggest that you ask the boss to reschedule the meeting so you can eat your chocolate chip cookies!) Eat your snack before or after the meeting, but be sure to allow yourself the time to eat it slowly, whichever time you choose.

On the other hand, if your peak period happens to coincide with a regular date with friends, bring your snack with you and explain what you are doing. In fact, if you and your friends get together every afternoon for coffee and cake, your snack can be your substitute for their cake.

When You Forget

Our memories being what they are, it is a safe bet that sooner or later you and your snack will be in two different places. Since it is unlikely that you will have your snack list with you, you'll have to guess at what an appropriate snack would be. Generally speaking, you can assume that the following snacks fall into the acceptable carbohydrate and calorie range: most 1-ounce candy bars or bags of chips; a plain doughnut, a muffin, a packaged slice of cake, brownie, or cookies.

When you get home, look up the calorie and carbohydrate content of the snack that you ate so you can decide whether or not to eat it in the next emergency. Many vending machine cookies and brownies contain about 250 calories and about 35 grams of carbohydrate. The extra calories won't make much difference to your diet if you forget your snack very occasionally; however, don't let your love of brownies make you "forget" every day.

On the Road with Your Snack

Whenever possible, take your snacks with you when you travel, especially when you are out of the country. Changes in time, in when and what you eat, and the presence of mouth-watering pastry shops on every corner make you especially vulnerable to any whipped-cream-filled chocolate-covered confection that you see. If you are traveling abroad and run out of snacks, save a roll and jam from breakfast to eat later on. If you forget your snack when traveling in this country, follow the instructions in the preceding paragraphs.

The mere fact of travel offers some problems for the snacking dieter. Jet lag, interestingly enough, can alter the time you want to snack. If you are traveling from east to west, say, from Boston to Los Angeles, you may experience a profound desire for carbohydrate when your body clock says it is time for sleep and the electric clock says it's too early. Ignore the craving. It is your body's way of getting you to go to sleep. It will go away when you have adjusted to the new time schedule.

Avoiding the Binge

A common fear among people who start the Carbohydrate Craver's Diet is that one snack won't be enough. One snack will just set them off; before they know it, they'll have eaten the week's supply.

It is true that, in the beginning, you may not find the immediate carbohydrate gratification that you will get after a while. For the most part, that is because you eat your snacks too quickly. You not only eat them too quickly, you expect to feel carbohydrate-full the minute you've swallowed that last bite. But if you had a headache and took an aspirin, you wouldn't expect the headache to disappear the minute you swallowed the pill; you'd give it twenty minutes or a half-hour. It's the same with the carbohydrate-serotonin connection; it takes a little while for it to work.

The obvious difference here is that you aren't going to be tempted to binge on aspirin, whereas you might on carbohydrates. So, if the problem should arise — and don't expect that it automatically will — here's how to deal with it.

When you begin the diet, keep only one snack readily available. Store the others in an inconvenient and somewhat inaccessible spot. When the craving period arrives, make yourself something to drink — if you are at work, buy something — and find a comfortable place to sit. Make a note of the time. And then begin to eat. Very slowly. Take at least ten minutes to finish off the snack, more if possible. Sip your beverage, talk, read, watch television, or look out the window. You can go on to doing something else after fifteen minutes have passed, but don't go near any food.

When thirty minutes have passed since you first started to eat, ask yourself if you are as hungry for carbohydrates as you were a half-hour earlier. Be sure to distinguish between a desire to *taste* more of the snack and a need actually to consume it. You should feel a lessening of the carbohydrate hunger. It may not be entirely gone, but the urgency to eat carbohydrate should be stilled.

Tell yourself that tomorrow (and tomorrow) you will be able to eat the snack again. You can eat it or another like it for as long as you want.

If you still feel a longing for more carbohydrate after all of this, then get another snack and repeat the same procedure. During the first few days of the diet, your body may need more carbohydrate at snack time, especially if you had been denying yourself carbohydrate before you started on the diet. This excessive need will pass, and by the end of the first week you will be satisfied with one snack during each craving period. Don't worry about the extra calories in the second snack; your ability to stick to the diet will offset them.

One of my patients told me, "I really never thought it would work. I was sure that I would eat the entire bag of candy bars. In the past, I couldn't rest until I had polished off any candy I knew was somewhere in the house. But now, knowing I had to eat the candy every day removed that compulsion to eat it all at once."

———

After following this procedure for about a week, you will become sensitive to the feeling of carbohydrate hunger before snacking and to carbohydrate satisfaction after snacking. When you are convinced that eating carbohydrate takes away the hunger for more, you can stop following such a rigid snacking procedure and bring the rest of the snacks back into the house or office. Always eat the snacks slowly, however. That should never change.

Snacks by Carbohydrate Content

STARCHY SNACKS

SNACK	AMOUNT	CARBO-HYDRATE (grams)	CALORIES
Wasa Crisp Bread, Hearty Rye	6 crackers	**66**	192

SNACK	AMOUNT	CARBO-HYDRATE (*grams*)	CALORIES
RyKrisp	6 triple crackers	54	180
Wasa Crisp Bread, Sport	5 crackers	45	200
Rice crackers, plain, or any flavor	10	44	200
Melba toast	13 slices	43	199
Mister Salty Veri-Thin pretzel sticks (Nabisco)	2 ounces	42	200
Mister Salty Veri-Thin pretzel (Nabisco), 3-ring variety	18 small	41	198
English muffin (Thomas' or Wonder), plus 1 tablespoon non-diet jelly	1	41	183
Wasa Crisp Bread, Golden Rye	5 crackers	40	195
Ideal Flatbread	5 crackers	40	170
Rice cakes (25 calories per cake)	8	40	200
Rice cakes (36 calories per cake)	5	38	180

SNACK	AMOUNT	CARBO-HYDRATE (*grams*)	CALORIES
Popcorn, no butter	3½ cups	37	189
Matzo, plus 1 tablespoon nondiet jelly	1	37	167
Graham crackers, plain or honey	7 single crackers	37	167
Egg Jumbo (Stella D'oro)	4	36.5	176
Corn muffin, average size, with 1 tablespoon nondiet jelly	1	36	191
Blueberry muffin rounds, frozen (Morton), with 1 tablespoon nondiet jelly	1	36	160
Cinnamon toast	4	35	196
Barnum's Animal Crackers (Nabisco)	17	33	200
Zwieback	6	32	192
Bran muffin, average size, with 1 tablespoon nondiet jelly	1	32	154
Saltines	14	32	196
Uneeda Biscuits	9	32	189
Butter Thins Crackers	11	31	198

SNACK	AMOUNT	CARBO-HYDRATE (*grams*)	CALORIES
Soda Crackers (Sunshine)	10	**30**	200
Bagel, average size, with 1 tablespoon diet margarine	1	**30**	200
Wheat Thins (Nabisco)	22	**27**	198
Bread sticks (Stella D'oro), sesame	4	**27**	212
Waverly Thins	11	**27**	198
Chocolate Grahams (Nabisco)	3	**27**	208
French fried potatoes	2 ounces	**26**	187
Bread sticks (Stella D'oro), plain	4	**26**	164
Cheese Nips Crackers (Nabisco)	38	**25**	200
Better Cheddars Snack Thins (Nabisco)	30	**25**	200

SWEET SNACKS

SNACK	AMOUNT	CARBO-HYDRATE (*grams*)	CALORIES
M & M's Plain Chocolate Candies	1.4-ounce package	55	201
M & M's, Royals Mint Chocolate	1.26-ounce package	55	182
Butter Mints and Party Mints (Kraft)	2 ounces	51	208
Marshmallows (try them toasted)	8	50	200
Jelly beans	30 (3 ounces)	50	198
Popsicle	3 single	50	195
Pixy Stix (Sunline Brands)	2 servings	50	200
Chuckles Jelly Candy (Nabisco)	5 pieces (2-ounce package)	50	200
Gumdrops	2 ounces	49	198
Popsicle, Kool-Pop	8	48	192
Popsicle, Twin-Pop	2 bars	47	190
Fudgsicle	2	47	204
Spearmint Leaves (Brach)	7	47	189

SNACK	AMOUNT	CARBO-HYDRATE (grams)	CALORIES
Orange Slices (Brach)	3	47	192
Jelly Nougat (Brach)	5	45	200
Saltwater Taffy, all flavors (Brach)	5	44	200
Big Ben Jellies (Brach)	6	43	174
Red Twist (Brach)	2 ounces	43	198
Golden Fruit Raisin Biscuits (Sunshine)	3	43	183
Dixie Vanilla (Sunshine)	3	43	180
Fig Bars (Sunshine)	4	41	180
Orange and Brach Perkys	3	41	165
Wrapped Chocolates, Orange, Raspberry, Vanilla, Maple (Brach)	3	41	192
Chocolate Covered Mint Creme (Brach)	3	41	195
Licorice Twist (Brach)	2 ounces	40	186

SNACK	AMOUNT	CARBO-HYDRATE (grams)	CALORIES
Good and Fruity	1 package	40	160
Charleston Chew (Nabisco)	1¾-ounce bar	40	200
Sherbet, orange	6 ounces (¾ cup)	40	180
Bordeaux Cookies (Pepperidge Farm)	8	40	192
Aunt Sally Iced Cookies (Sunshine)	2	40	198
Frozen yogurt (Lite-line, Borden)	7 ounces	39	194
Summit cookie bar	1 package	39	194
Anisette Sponge (Stella D'oro)	4	39	196
Frozen yogurt (Strawberry Bar)	3 bars	38	207
Milk Chocolate Covered Cherries (Brach)	3	38	198
Chocolate Treat or Vanilla Treat, frozen confection on stick (Weight Watchers)	2	38	200
Gingersnaps	12	38	199

SNACK	AMOUNT	CARBO-HYDRATE (*grams*)	CALORIES
Bit-O-Honey	1 bar (1.7 ounces)	38	188
Good and Plenty	1 package	37	151
MalloPuffs (Sunshine)	3	37	199
Molasses and Spice Cookies (Sunshine)	3	36	201
Lady fingers	4 large	36	200
Milkmaid Caramel (Brach)	5	36	200
Wrapped Chocolates, Cherry Nougat (Brach)	3	35	174
Caramels, plain or chocolate	5 pieces (1½ ounces)	35	188
Chocolate Snaps (Sunshine)	16	35	208
Anisette Toast (Stella D'oro)	4	35	172
Pfeffernusse Spice Drops (Stella D'oro)	5	34	180
Iced Oatmeal Cookies (Sunshine)	3	34	207
Sprinkles (Sunshine)	3	34	171
Pop-Tarts (Kellogg), any flavor	1	34	200
Social Tea Biscuits (Nabisco)	9	34	193

SNACK	AMOUNT	CARBO-HYDRATE (*grams*)	CALORIES
Sugar Daddy Milk Caramel Pop	1 lollipop (1⅜ ounces)	33	185
Sugared Egg Biscuits (Stella D'oro)	3	33	192
Assorted Royals (Brach)	6	33	180
Butter Thin Cookies (Rich)	4	32	200
Milky Way Snack Bar	2	32	200
Pudding Pops, frozen (Jell-O), vanilla, banana, or chocolate	2	32	200
Ruffelo frozen ice-milk sandwich	2	32	160
Cream Lunch (Sunshine)	4	32	180
Brownie Nut Snack Bar (Pepperidge Farm)	1	31	190
Raisin Spice Snack Bar (Pepperidge Farm)	1	31	170

SNACK	AMOUNT	CARBO-HYDRATE (*grams*)	CALORIES
Breakfast Treats (Stella D'oro)	2	31	210
Piccolo Rolled Wafers (Nabisco)	9	31	189
Assorted Toffees (Brach)	6	30	180
Devil's Food Cupcake (Hostess)	1	30	185
Chocolate Sundae (Dairy Queen)	1 small	30	170
Ice milk, vanilla, strawberry	7 ounces	29	190
Date Nut Snack Bar (Pepperidge Farm)	1	29	160
Granola Clusters (Nature Valley), almond, caramel, raisin	1 cluster	28	150
3 Musketeers Snack Bar	2	28	160
Crumb cake, blueberry, cherry, French	1 cake	28	175
Orbit Creme Sandwich (Sunshine)	4	28	204

SNACK	AMOUNT	CARBO-HYDRATE (*grams*)	CALORIES
Vanilla Wafers (Sunshine)	13	28	195
Hydrox (Sunshine), mint, vanilla, regular	4	28	200
Butter-Flavored Cookies (Sunshine)	8	28	192
Brown Edge Wafers (Nabisco)	7	28	196
Fig Pastry (Stella D'oro)	2	28	190
Ice-cream sandwich	1 (2⅓ ounces)	27	174
Morning Light Donuts, frozen (Morton), chocolate iced, glazed, jelly	1	26	200
Sugar Wafers (Sunshine), plain or lemon	4	26	176
Oatmeal Cookies (Sunshine)	3	26	174
Apple Pastry (Stella D'oro)	2	26	180
Prune Pastry (Stella D'oro)	2	26	180

Bongos, frozen chocolate- covered pops (Thin's Inn)	2	**26**	180

FRUIT SNACKS

SNACK	AMOUNT	CARBO- HYDRATE (*grams*)	CALORIES
Fresh Fruit			
Plums	6 medium	**53**	198
Apricots	8	**51**	200
Cherries	43 large	**50**	200
Peaches	5 medium	**48.5**	190
Tangerines	4 large	**46**	184
Green grapes	63 medium	**45**	200
Banana	1 large	**44**	170
Strawberries	3½ cups	**44**	200
Navel oranges	2 medium	**35.5**	142
Apple	1 large	**33**	133
Pear	1 medium	**31**	122
Dried Fruit			
Banana flakes	5 ounces	**56**	200
Raisins	4 ounces	**55**	205
Dates, pitted	7 medium	**53**	200
Apricots	13	**51**	200
Prunes	4	**45**	200
Figs	3 medium	**41**	164
Apple, unsweet- ened	1 cup	**41**	200

6

The Super Salads

BOTH of the Carbohydrate Craver's Diets — the Basic and the Dense — include a Super Salad that must be eaten every day. This salad is the nutritional foundation of the diet. For a mere 75 to 80 calories, it supplies all your vitamin A and C and folic acid needs — saving enough calories to allow you to eat your carbohydrate snack every day.

You may eat the whole salad at one meal or divide it in half and eat it at both lunch and dinner. But you must eat it. And please make and eat just the amount called for. Unlike other diets, which give you unlimited portions of salad (hoping you'll feel too full to notice your carbohydrate hunger), the Carbohydrate Craver's Diet plan does not permit unlimited amounts of anything. Even vegetable calories add up. There is one exception and that is parsley, which is the main component of the three Super Salads. Parsley is packed with vitamins A and C and folic acid — just 1 ounce contains almost all your daily requirements for these vitamins — and all for 12 calories. So if you want to double the amount of parsley, or munch on a handful during the day, that's fine.

In the beginning, you'll need to use your kitchen scale to weigh out the amount of parsley in 1 ounce; pretty soon, you'll learn to estimate the right amount, just as you will with other foods that you use regularly. Both the tops and the stems are nutritious, and if you don't want to eat the stems in your salads, save them for soup; keep them in a plastic bag in the freezer. Curly parsley and flat Italian parsley are equally nutritious and equally low in calories. Use whichever you prefer.

Three salads are offered: Super Standard Salad, Super Spinach-Mushroom Salad, and Super Cole-slaw. The most important component of each is parsley. Low-calorie salad dressing or mayonnaise is included in the salad recipes. Use any commercial dressing or mayonnaise that contains 25 calories or fewer per tablespoon. If you like, you can substitute lemon juice or rice vinegar (a very mild vinegar) for the dressing and save some calories. However, lemon juice and vinegar may make your stomach feel acidic and mimic hunger pains, so avoid them if they do.

Shopping for your salad components should become second nature, part of your regular weekly shopping expedition. To make life easier for yourself, you can make up several days' worth of salad ingredients ahead of time, and package the right quantity for one salad in a plastic bag. If you eat one meal a day out, eat all of your salad at the other meal — or take the salad with you.

Still, there are certain to be some times when you cannot get the ingredients (or find the place) to eat your salad. On those days, you'll have to get your vitamins from other sources. The following are reasonably low-calorie substitutes, which will provide for your daily needs:

Vitamin C (choose *one*)
1 orange
½ grapefruit
1 cup strawberries
6 ounces cut-up citrus fruit (¾ cup)

Vitamin A and Folic Acid (choose *one*)
1 carrot and 1 cup romaine lettuce
¾ cup chopped kale or other greens
4 ounces (raw weight) asparagus
3 stalks broccoli

The Salads

SUPER STANDARD SALAD
1 ounce parsley, chopped
½ medium red or green pepper, chopped
½ cup red or green cabbage, chopped or shredded
1 small carrot, sliced, shredded, or chopped

½ cup scallions, onions, celery, or cucumber, chopped (optional)

1 cup alfalfa or bean sprouts (optional)

1 tablespoon diet Italian salad dressing (optional)

SUPER MUSHROOM-SPINACH SALAD

2 ounces parsley, chopped

3½ ounces fresh spinach, chopped (or ½ cellophane bag)

4 large or 10 small fresh mushrooms, sliced

1 tablespoon soybean "bacon bits" (optional)

1 tablespoon diet Italian salad dressing (optional)

SUPER COLESLAW

2 ounces parsley, chopped

1 cup red or green cabbage, chopped

1 small carrot, shredded or chopped

½ cup scallions, onions, celery, or cucumber, chopped (optional)

2 tablespoons fresh dill, chopped (optional)

1 tablespoon diet mayonnaise (optional)

7

The Carbohydrate Craver's Basic Diet

THE CARBOHYDRATE CRAVER'S Basic Diet supplies 900 calories a day in meals and 200 calories a day in a carbohydrate-rich snack. Breakfast provides 200 calories, lunch 300, and dinner 400.

Select the components of each meal from the breakfast, lunch, and dinner food exchange lists, or follow the menus for each of these meals. The menus can be used in any order and, unless otherwise indicated, the same menu can be used for as long as you wish. Do not eliminate any items on the menus or replace them with other foods. The menus were developed to provide the correct amount of vitamins, minerals, and protein for a particular meal, and if you make substitutions, you risk altering the meal's nutrient content.

If at all possible, eat one of the Super Salads each day. If necessary, however, you can substitute a fruit or vegetable from the list in Chapter 6 for the salad twice a week. Don't do this more frequently because the Super Salads contain a larger variety of vitamins than any one fruit or vegetable. Drink the recommended servings of milk or eat the other dairy products listed in the food lists or in the menus. If you do not wish to include these foods at meals, eat them at some other time.

The recipes are designed to be compatible with a variety of cooking styles. Some are more adaptable to family cooking, others to eating alone. Try to minimize the time you spend in the kitchen by cooking enough to last for three meals. Chicken and rice both lend themselves to this time-saving cookery and can be incorporated into lunch and dinner menus.

At the end of the Carbohydrate Craver's Basic Diet you'll find a list of low-calorie, frozen-dinner entrees and the additional foods necessary to complete the nutritional adequacy of these meals. These frozen dinners are useful when you must prepare something for your family that is too fattening for you to eat on the diet plan or if you lack time or motivation to cook dinner.

Certain foods appear with great regularity on the diet program: the Super Salads, dairy products, water-packed tuna fish, whole-wheat Syrian bread pockets, potatoes, and rice. These foods are good sources of nutrients, low in fat, and generally considered palatable by most people (although long-term dieters may wonder if there is life after tuna fish). Teach yourself to buy them automatically when you do your weekly shopping. They are also nutritionally worthwhile foods for you to eat after you complete the diet.

If you are the sort of person who knows a week in advance exactly what meals you are going to serve on which day, you don't need any advice on shopping for the diets. But if you are the kind who wanders into the supermarket at 5:45, wondering what to eat for dinner, you should duplicate the menu pages and stuff them into your briefcase or handbag or pocket.

Several menus require no more preparation time than opening a few cans and mixing their contents together in a pot. If you don't like to cook any meat, buy lean roast beef or barbecued chicken from the deli counter of the supermarket. If the only vegetables you eat are the kind that garnish a Big Mac, explore the freezer chest of the supermarket to learn what is available already peeled, sliced, and precooked. Avoid any vegetables with fancy pictures on the box showing them coated with sauce.

A list of optional seasonings is given in several recipes. Do not feel limited by this list. Vary the taste of your dishes by adding condiments, herbs, and spices as you wish. However, use restraint in adding salty ingredients such as soy sauce or bouillon, or garlic, onion, or other seasoning salts. Experiment with seasonings that various ethnic cooks like to use, such as the peppery sauces used in Spanish cooking, the curries and cumin used in Middle Eastern and Indian cooking, and the fresh ginger and rice vinegar used in Oriental cooking.

In recipes that call for cooking without oil or in a nonstick utensil, spray your pan with nonstick spray or use a Teflon- or SilverStone-coated pan.

In recipes that call for broth, use canned or powdered broth, any flavor.

THE CARBOHYDRATE CRAVER'S BASIC DIET

Breakfast Exchange List

Eat *one* serving from the cereal *or* bread lists below, plus one cup of skim milk, ½ cup orange or grapefruit juice, and black coffee or tea or diet beverages as desired. Or follow one of the alternative breakfast menus. If you select the alternative menus, be sure not to eat eggs more than two or three times a week.

CEREALS

Bran Buds	½ cup
Bran Flakes	1 cup
Cheerios	1 cup
Cornflakes	1 cup
Grape-nuts Flakes	1 cup

Hot cereal, cooked	½ cup
Life	⅔ cup
Most	½ cup
Product 19	1 cup
Puffed Rice or Puffed Wheat	2 cups (these tend to get soggy when milk is added so consider eating the cereal with your fingers and drinking the milk)
Rice Krispies	1 cup
Shredded Wheat	1 biscuit
Total (corn)	⅔ cup
Wheat Chex	⅔ cup
Wheaties	1 cup

BREADS

1 slice whole-wheat bread
½ bagel, any flavor, regular size
½ English muffin
½ large bran muffin
4 rice cakes

You may use 1 tablespoon of diet jelly or 1 tablespoon of diet margarine with any of these selections.

Alternative Breakfast Menus

1 waffle or pancake, frozen
½ cup 1 percent fat cottage cheese
¾ cup strawberries *or* ½ cup blueberries *or*
  ½ grapefruit

1 egg, boiled or cooked without oil
4 slices Melba toast
1 cup skim milk

1 sausage link
1 egg, boiled or cooked without oil
1 cup skim milk

1 egg scrambled with ½ slice cheese, cooked
  without oil
2 slices Melba toast
½ cup skim milk

½ toasted English muffin
1 slice lean ham
½ cup skim milk

Lunch Exchange List

Eat *one* food from each of the categories given
below, or follow one of the lunch menu plans in its
entirety. Black coffee or tea or diet beverages as
desired.

PROTEIN-RICH FOODS

2 ounces chicken or turkey, cooked or raw weight (white meat only, no skin)

2 ounces tuna fish, packed in water

1½ ounces very lean packaged cold cuts (Check calories on label if possible: Buddig and Best Kosher are good choices.)

⅔ cup 1 percent fat cottage cheese

BREAD

1 3-inch-diameter whole-wheat Syrian bread pocket

1 slice rye or whole-wheat or multigrain bread

½ bagel (normal size)

½ English muffin (whole wheat, if available)

SPREADS

(This category may be omitted and replaced with an additional choice of dairy foods.)

1 tablespoon diet mayonnaise

1 tablespoon diet margarine

1 tablespoon diet Italian salad dressing

DAIRY FOODS

4 ounces skim milk (no fat)

1 slice Lite-line cheese

½ ounce skim-milk mozzarella cheese
⅓ cup 1 percent fat cottage cheese
⅓ cup plain low-fat yogurt

FRUIT* OR VEGETABLES

½ portion of any Super Salad
¾ cup strawberries
½ cup blueberries
1 small orange
⅓ medium-sized cantaloupe

Lunch Menus

Sandwich Lunches

EGG SALAD SANDWICH

2 hard-boiled eggs, chopped
½ green pepper
1 stalk celery
1 scallion or ¼ onion, to taste
1 tablespoon diet mayonnaise
1 3-inch-diameter Syrian bread pocket, preferably whole wheat

Eat with:

½ cup skim milk

---

*Do not choose fruit more than twice a week.

BAGEL AND CHEESE

   1 bagel, regular size

   1 slice Swiss, Münster, American, or skim-milk mozzarella cheese

   mustard or 1 teaspoon diet mayonnaise or diet margarine

Eat with:

   1 green pepper

CLUB SANDWICH

   2 ounces cold chicken or turkey, sliced

   2 slices tomato

   1 teaspoon imitation soybean "bacon bits" mixed with 1 teaspoon diet mayonnaise

   lettuce

   2 slices whole-wheat bread

Eat with:

   ½ cup skim milk

TUNA FISH SANDWICH

   1 3½-ounce can water-packed tuna (or canned chicken)

   onion, chopped, to taste

   1 stalk celery

   shredded lettuce

   fresh dill

   alfalfa sprouts

   1 tablespoon diet mayonnaise

Put into a 3-inch-diameter Syrian bread pocket

Eat with:

> ½ cup skim milk

COLD CUTS

> 2½ ounces lean cold cuts (read the label —
> should not contain more than 125 calories
> each serving; Buddig and Best Kosher are
> good choices)
> 1 pickle, chopped
> catsup and mustard, to taste

Put into a 3-inch-diameter Syrian bread pocket

Eat with:

> 1 small orange *or* ¾ cup strawberries
> ½ cup skim milk

Salad Lunches

WINTER SALAD

> 1 cup 1 percent fat cottage cheese
> 1 green pepper, sliced or chopped
> 1 cucumber
> fresh dill, if available
> 1 scallion (optional)
> salt, pepper, or seasoning salt to taste

Eat with:

> 1 English muffin *or* 1 piece matzo *or* 1 3-inch-diameter Syrian bread pocket

SUMMER SALAD

> 1 cup 1 percent fat cottage cheese
> ⅓ medium-sized cantaloupe, sliced
> ½ cup blueberries *or* ½ cup strawberries

Top with two frozen cubes of low-calorie cranberry juice

Eat with:

> 1 3-inch-diameter Syrian bread pocket *or* two large rice crackers

GREEK SALAD

> 1 serving any Super Salad
> 1 ounce feta cheese
> 1 hard-boiled egg *or* 1-ounce slice lean ham *or* turkey *or* chicken
> 1 tablespoon diet Italian salad dressing

Eat with:

> 1 3-inch-diameter Syrian bread pocket

Weekend Lunches

    1 slice French toast, frozen
    1-ounce slice lean ham
    1 ounce Swiss cheese

Put the ham and cheese on the French toast and put under broiler until cheese melts.

Eat with:

    ½ cup skim milk

---

    3 fish sticks, baked or warmed in nonstick pan

Eat with:

    ½ serving any Super Salad
    1 cup skim milk

---

    1 tortilla shell filled with:
    1 ounce chicken *or* water-packed tuna, chopped
    1 ounce parsley
    1 small tomato, chopped
    ½ green pepper, chopped
    onion to taste
    ½ slice cheese, crumbled
    hot sauce to taste

Eat with:

    ½ cup skim milk

---

2 slices whole-wheat or rye bread covered
    with:
1 ounce any meltable hard cheese
1 slice tomato
2 teaspoons soybean "bacon bits"
1 tablespoon diet mayonnaise or mustard

Put under broiler until cheese is melted.

Dinner Exchange List

Choose *one* food from each of the categories given
below, or follow one of the suggested dinner menu
plans. Black coffee or tea or diet beverages as desired.

PROTEIN-RICH FOODS

(Unless otherwise stated, all weights are raw
weight.)

FISH
5 ounces carp
6 ounces cod
7 ounces haddock
5 ounces halibut
3½ ounces herring
5 ounces pike
5 ounces pollock

3 ounces rainbow trout
5 ounces salmon
7 ounces sole
7 ounces squid
5 ounces striped bass
4 ounces swordfish
4 ounces tuna fish, canned, packed in water

SHELLFISH
¾ cup (2½ ounces) clams, canned, drained
7 ounces clams (8 large or 18 small)
¾ cup (4½ ounces) crabmeat, canned
1 cup (5½ ounces) lobster, cooked
7 ounces oysters, canned
5 ounces oysters, raw westerns, or 4 oysters
5 ounces shrimp

MEAT AND POULTRY
2½ ounces very lean beef, cooked, all fat
  trimmed
3½ ounces beef or chicken liver
3 ounces chicken or turkey, cooked (white
  meat only, no skin)
2 ounces lamb chop, trimmed, cooked
3 ounces lean leg of lamb, roasted
2 ounces pork chop, very lean, cooked
2½ ounces pork, very lean, roasted
2½ ounces veal, cooked

CHEESE
- 1 cup 1 percent fat cottage cheese
- 2 ounces skim-milk mozzarella cheese

BREAD AND OTHER STARCHY FOODS

- 1 slice whole-wheat, rye, or multigrain bread
- 1 3-inch-diameter Syrian bread pocket
- 1 tortilla
- ½ cup rice (converted or brown), cooked
- ½ cup pasta, cooked
- ½ cup potatoes, mashed
- 1 medium-sized potato (about 3 ounces), baked or boiled

SALADS

- 1 serving any Super Salad (or eat ½ serving for dinner and ½ for lunch)

DAIRY FOODS

- ½ cup skim milk (no fat)
- 1 slice Lite-line cheese
- ⅓ cup 1 percent fat cottage cheese
- ½ ounce skim-milk mozzarella cheese
- ⅓ cup plain low-fat yogurt

VEGETABLES

(Unless otherwise stated, measurements are for cooked vegetables.)

1 cup (4 ounces) asparagus

1 cup beans, green, cooked or raw

1 cup beans, wax

½ cup beets

1 cup or 4 ounces broccoli

⅔ cup Brussels sprouts

½ cup cabbage, red

1 cup cabbage, regular, cooked or raw

1 cup carrots or 1 large raw carrot

1 cup cauliflower

½ cup collard greens, turnip greens, dandelion greens, beet greens, or Swiss chard (These vegetables tend to look like overgrown weeds in the produce section, but they are extremely nutritious. They are also available in the frozen-food section. Cook them like spinach.)

¾ cup kale

1 cup raw lettuce, romaine (add to Super Salad if desired)

1 large pepper, green

1 cup spinach

1 cup squash, summer (yellow) or zucchini (green)

1 cup tomatoes, stewed

FRUIT

2 medium-sized apricots, fresh

3 medium-sized apricots, canned, packed in water

½ cup blueberries

⅓ medium-sized cantaloupe, 5-inch diameter
(You don't have to take a tape measure to
the supermarket — you can spot a medium-
sized melon.)

½ medium-sized grapefruit, 4-inch diameter

½ cup grapefruit segments, canned, packed
in water

¼ medium-sized honeydew melon, 5-inch
diameter

1 large nectarine

1 small orange

½ cup orange sections

1 medium-sized peach, fresh

½ cup pineapple, fresh

2 medium-sized purple plums, canned,
packed in water

¾ cup strawberries

1 medium-sized tangelo

2 small tangerines

¾ cup watermelon

Dinner Menus

BAKED FISH I

> 5 ounces flounder *or* haddock *or* 3 ounces other white fish
>
> 1 ounce meltable cheese (Swiss, skim-milk mozzarella, cheddar)
>
> seasoning salt or powdered vegetable broth, any flavor
>
> 1 tablespoon diet margarine

Sprinkle the cheese and seasoning over the fish. Dot with diet margarine and bake in 350 °F oven for 15 to 20 minutes or until done.

Eat with:

> 1 cup broccoli seasoned with soy sauce, sesame seeds, rice vinegar, cumin, or fresh dill
>
> 1 medium potato (baked or boiled) *or* ½ cup rice, cooked in broth, sprinkled with nutmeg

Add 1 tablespoon chopped parsley to rice or potato or eat it while preparing meal.

BAKED FISH II

> 4 ounces haddock *or* 2 ounces mackerel *or* 3 ounces bluefish *or* 3 ounces other white fish
>
> 1 tablespoon soy sauce *or* teriyaki sauce
>
> 1 teaspoon garlic, fresh, chopped
>
> ginger, chopped fresh (optional), to taste

Pour soy sauce, garlic, and ginger over fish. Cover and bake in 350°F oven for 15 to 20 minutes or until done.

Eat with:

> 1 cup Brussels sprouts cooked in broth with a little rice vinegar or lemon juice
>
> 1 serving any Super Salad
>
> ½ cup rice, brown or converted

POT ROAST

> 4 ounces lean brisket (or lean steak)
>
> 1 cup broth *or* 1 cup tomato juice
>
> 1 tablespoon onions, chopped
>
> ½ teaspoon garlic
>
> ½ teaspoon ginger (or other spices, such as paprika, chili, or oregano)

Sear the meat briefly in a nonstick pan. Add the broth, mixed with the onion, garlic, and spices, and simmer until done.

Eat with:

> 1 medium-sized potato garnished with green onion, chives, fresh dill, pepper, or lemon salt
>
> 1 cup beets, fresh or canned, with seasoning salt and lemon juice
>
> ½ cup skim milk

BAKED CHICKEN

3½ ounces baked chicken (without skin and bones)

In order to make enough chicken for 3 or more meals, bake a whole chicken, then remove skin and bones; weigh and refrigerate or freeze remainder. Try sprinkling dry salad dressing or onion soup mix on chicken before baking.

Eat with:

1 cup carrots, raw or cooked in small amount of broth, with fresh dill

1 medium-sized potato, baked or boiled

1 serving any Super Salad

CURRIED CHICKEN

3½ ounces chicken breast (without skin and bones)

1 teaspoon cooking oil

½ onion, chopped

1 stalk celery, sliced

2 cloves garlic, crushed

½ teaspoon curry powder
coriander, cumin (optional), to taste

⅓ cup plain low-fat yogurt

Sauté chicken in oil with onion, celery, garlic, and seasonings. When cooked through, add the yogurt and heat gently (to prevent yogurt from curdling) over low heat until warm.

Eat with:

> ½ cup cooked rice *or* ½ cup cooked orzo
> (rice-shaped macaroni)
> 1 serving any Super Salad

TOMATOED CHICKEN

> ½ green pepper
> ½ onion
> 2 cloves garlic, fresh, crushed
> 1 teaspoon cooking oil
> ½ cup tomato purée
> ½ cup mushrooms
> 3½ ounces baked chicken (without skin and
> bones)
> oregano, basil, thyme, fennel seeds, or
> crushed red pepper, to taste

Sauté green pepper, onion, and garlic in cooking oil, then add remaining ingredients, except the chicken, and simmer 5 minutes. Add the chicken and cook for another 5 minutes.

Eat with:

> ½ cup cooked rice *or* 1 medium-sized potato
> *or* ½ cup cooked macaroni
> ½ cup skim milk

FAST TOMATOED CHICKEN

3½ ounces baked chicken (without skin and
bones) added to ½ 10-ounce can zucchini in
tomato sauce

Eat with:

½ cup cooked pasta *or* ½ cup instant rice
1 serving any Super Salad

CHEESE-SPINACH CASSEROLE

½ package spinach, frozen (thawed in refrigerator and drained)
1 egg, beaten
2 tablespoons (1 ounce) hard cheese, grated
or chopped
½ cup skim milk
2 slices whole-wheat bread, toasted and cut
into cubes
salt and pepper to taste
pinch nutmeg* *or* one or more of the following: curry, chili, cumin, cayenne pepper, or
Tabasco sauce, to taste

Mix all the ingredients together and pour them into
a nonstick baking dish. Bake in 350°F oven for 30
minutes. The dish may be prepared in the morning
and heated in the oven just before serving.

---

*Nutmeg graters allow you to grate a few sprinkles of fresh
nutmeg for a stronger but less bitter taste than that of dry
nutmeg. Nutmeg lasts for years.

TUNA FISH CASSEROLE

1 3½-ounce can tuna fish, water packed
½ cup plain low-fat yogurt
½ cup carrots, cooked
1 cup noodles, cooked
scallions, celery, fresh dill, or chives)
  (optional)
any combination of seasoning salt, lemon salt,
  Worcestershire sauce, Tabasco sauce, chili,
  curry, dry or prepared mustard, or sesame
  seeds, to taste

Mix everything together and cook in heavy-bottom
pot over medium heat for about 15 minutes.

Eat with:

1 serving any Super Salad

FISH NEWBURG

5 ounces shrimp *or* halibut *or* 3 ounces any
  other white fish
½ cup plain low-fat yogurt
¼ cup skim milk
1 teaspoon catsup
1 tablespoon sherry (optional)
1 ounce (2 tablespoons) chopped parsley
pinch cayenne or drop Tabasco sauce

Bake the fish in 350°F oven for 25 minutes or until
shrimp is pink or fish flakes to the fork. Place the
cooked fish in a saucepan and pour all the remain-

ing ingredients over it. Warm gently (to prevent yogurt from curdling) over low heat for 5 minutes.

Eat with:

> 1 cup cooked spinach
> 1 serving any Super Salad

SEAFOOD CASSEROLE

> 2 ounces shrimp, cooked, *or* 2 ounces scallops, raw, *or* 2 ounces haddock, cooked, *or* 2½ ounces any other white fish, cooked
> ½ cup plain low-fat yogurt
> ¼ cup skim milk
> 1 tablespoon onion powder *or* ¼ onion *or* 2 scallions, chopped
> 2 tablespoons parsley, chopped
> ½ ounce (2 tablespoons or ½ slice) hard cheese
> 2 cloves garlic, fresh, crushed or chopped
> 1 tablespoon sherry
> salt, pepper, cayenne, and Worcestershire sauce to taste

Mix all the ingredients and put them into a casserole. Bake in 350°F oven for 30 minutes.

Eat with:

> 1 serving any Super Salad

Quick Home Meals

What the following recipes lack in style, taste, or originality, they make up in speed of preparation and easy clean-up.

SOUP WITH BEEF

>   2 ounces lean hamburger
>   1 teaspoon cooking oil
>   1 10-ounce can Campbell Chunky Beef with Vegetable Soup

Brown the meat in the oil in a deep pot, add the soup to the pot, and heat it up.

Eat with:

>   1 serving any Super Salad

SUPERMARKET STEW

>   1 cup (8-ounce can) beef and vegetable stew spices to taste
>   1 slice whole-wheat toast, cut into triangles

Heat the stew and pour it over the toast points.

Eat with:

>   1 serving any Super Salad
>   ½ cup skim milk

SUPERMARKET CLAM CHOWDER

⅔ 10-ounce can frozen condensed New England–style clam chowder *or* 1 10-ounce can Manhattan-style clam chowder
½ cup canned clams, drained
1 cup skim milk
15 oyster crackers
paprika and pepper, to taste

Mix all the ingredients together and heat. Sprinkle the oyster crackers on top of the hot chowder.

Eat with:

1 serving any Super Salad

SUPERMARKET CORNED BEEF HASH

½ cup (½ 110-gram can) corned beef hash
1 egg

Cook the hash and the egg, without oil, side by side in the same pan. To serve, put the egg on top of the hash.

Eat with:

1 tablespoon catsup (optional)
1 serving any Super Salad
1 cup skim milk

CHEESEBURGER

3½ ounces lean hamburger patty
1 ounce cheese (American, Swiss, blue)

Brown the hamburger in a nonstick pan. Put the cheese on top until it melts.

Eat with:

> 1 toasted 3-inch-diameter Syrian bread pocket *or* ½ toasted English muffin
> 1 serving any Super Salad

HOT DOG AND SAUERKRAUT

> 1 all-beef hot dog (steamed, boiled, or pan fried without oil)
> ⅔ cup drained sauerkraut (to save a pan, warm the sauerkraut slightly with the hot dog)

Serve in a 3-inch-diameter Syrian bread pocket

Eat with:

> 1 cup skim milk
> 1 serving any Super Salad

SOUP AND POTATO

> 1 10¾-ounce can Campbell Chunky Sirloin Burger Soup
> ½ 1-pound can potatoes, drained
> 4 ounces green beans, cooked

Mix all together, warm, and serve.

Eat with:

> 1 serving any Super Salad

SAUCED PRECOOKED CHICKEN

> 2 ounces chicken *or* ham *or* turkey, canned or deli, cut up
> ½ 10-ounce can zucchini in tomato sauce
> oregano, basil, thyme, fennel, to taste

Mix all together, warm, and serve.

Eat with:

> ½ cup instant cooked rice
> 1 serving any Super Salad

The Least-Bother Meals

Low-calorie frozen main courses are now available and are extremely useful when time or inertia makes meal preparation too much of a bother. Because these dinners are not nutritionally complete, I suggest eating additional foods that contain the missing nutrients. They can be prepared while the dinner is warming up. If even this is too much bother, make sure that you add these side dishes to your menu for the next day, even if it means eating twice as much salad or drinking an extra cup of milk.

Weight Watchers

HADDOCK WITH STUFFING AND ITALIAN GREEN BEANS

Eat with:

> 1 serving any Super Salad
> 1 cup skim milk

SOLE IN LEMON SAUCE AND PEAS AND ONIONS

Eat with:

> 1 slice whole-wheat bread *or* ½ cup rice
> 1 serving any Super Salad
> ½ cup skim milk

CHICKEN LIVERS AND ONIONS

Eat with:

> 1 serving any Super Salad
> 1 cup skim milk

VEAL PATTY PARMIGIANA

Eat with:

> 1 serving any Super Salad
> 1 cup skim milk

ZITI MACARONI

Eat with:

> 1 serving any Super Salad

Stouffer's Lean Cuisine

CHICKEN CHOW MEIN WITH RICE

Eat with:

> 1 serving any Super Salad
> 1 cup skim milk

CHICKEN AND VEGETABLES WITH VERMICELLI

Eat with:

> ¼ cantaloupe *or* 1 cup strawberries
> 1 medium-sized peach *or* pear
> 1 cup skim milk

GLAZED CHICKEN WITH VEGETABLES AND RICE

Eat with:

> 1 small orange *or* ½ grapefruit
> 1 cup skim milk

FILET OF FISH DIVAN

Eat with:

> 1 slice whole-wheat bread *or* ½ cup rice
> 1 serving any Super Salad

FILET OF FISH FLORENTINE

Eat with:

> 1 slice whole-wheat bread
> 1 small orange *or* 1 cup strawberries
> 1 cup skim milk

MEATBALL STEW

Eat with:

> 1 serving any Super Salad
> 1 cup skim milk

ORIENTAL BEEF IN SAUCE WITH VEGETABLES

Eat with:

> 1 small orange *or* ½ cantaloupe *or* 1 cup
> strawberries
> 1 cup skim milk

ORIENTAL SCALLOPS, VEGETABLES, AND RICE

Eat with:

> 1 serving any Super Salad
> 1 cup skim milk

SPAGHETTI WITH BEEF AND MUSHROOM SAUCE

Eat with:

> 1 small orange *or* 1 cup strawberries
> 1 cup skim milk

ZUCCHINI LASAGNA

Eat with:

> 1 serving any Super Salad
> 1 slice whole-wheat bread
> 1 cup skim milk

8

The Carbohydrate Dense Diet

THE CARBOHYDRATE DENSE DIET supplies 900 calories a day in meals and 200 calories in a high-carbohydrate snack. The calories per meal are exactly the same as in the Basic Diet: 200 for breakfast, 300 for lunch, and 400 for dinner. This diet plan differs from the Basic Diet by supplying a larger amount of carbohydrate in each meal. If you compare the food lists for the Dense Diet with those of the Basic Diet, notice that the serving size of the bread and starchy food group is larger in this diet and the serving size of the protein foods slightly smaller. The amount of dairy products and fruits and vegetables allowed on the Dense Diet is the same as on the Basic Diet. Both diet plans are nutritionally adequate and, since they contain the same number of calories for each meal, can be interchanged.

The menu plans are useful in demonstrating ways in which high-carbohydrate foods can be incorporated into meals without sacrificing nutrition or adding calories. For the first two weeks, at least, you should follow the menu plans rather than the food exchange lists to learn how to combine ingredients to make these low-calorie–high-carbohydrate dishes. Then use the food lists to make up your own combinations.

Since the cooking time for the meals on the Carbohydrate Dense Diet is generally longer than for the Basic Diet, some advance planning is necessary. Try to cook the starchy component of the meal in the morning before you leave the house: Boil the rice or potato or cook the pasta. Although some of that freshly made quality will be lost, having these foods ready when you reenter the kitchen in the evening will prevent you from nibbling your way through a box of crackers while you are waiting for the water to boil. Making enough for two or three days is also a time saver.

Although rice is the only grain mentioned in the recipes, you can substitute equal amounts of other grains, such as buckwheat groats (kasha), barley, grits, millet, and wheat berries. If you do cook rice, use enriched converted rice or brown rice — they contain more nutrients than enriched white rice.

The pasta used in most of the menus is a protein-fortified brand call Superoni. Some of the flour used in regular pasta has been replaced by a protein-enriched powder, so the protein value of the pasta is similar to that of meat. It is made by the Prince Spaghetti Co., Lowell, Massachusetts; write to them if the product is not available in your area.

THE CARBOHYDRATE DENSE DIET

Breakfast Menus

Use the Breakfast Exchange List in Chapter 7, or the alternative menu plans suggested here. Black coffee or tea or diet beverages as desired.

½ cup plain low-fat yogurt
½ small banana (6 inches) *or* ½ cup blueberries *or* ¾ cup strawberries *or* ⅓ medium-sized cantaloupe

1 slice whole-wheat bread *or* 2 rice cakes
1 slice skim-milk mozzarella cheese, melted
½ cup skim milk

1 frozen waffle *or* 1 frozen pancake
1 tablespoon diet maple syrup
1 cup skim milk

½ toasted bagel
1 teaspoon peanut butter
1 teaspoon diet jelly
1 cup skim milk

1 matzo
1 teaspoon diet jelly
1 cup skim milk

Lunch Exchange List

Eat *one* food from each of the categories listed below or follow the suggested lunch menu plans. Black coffee or tea or diet beverages as desired.

PROTEIN-RICH FOODS

3 ounces shrimp, canned or fresh
1½ ounces water-packed tuna fish
1½ ounces very lean cold cuts (Buddig or Best Kosher, if possible)
1½ ounces turkey or chicken (white meat only, no skin)

BREADS

2 3-inch-diameter Syrian bread pockets
1 6-inch-diameter Syrian bread pocket
1 bagel, regular size
1 matzo
1 English muffin
2 slices whole-wheat, rye, or multigrain bread

SPREADS

(This category may be omitted and replaced with an additional choice of dairy foods.)

> 1 tablespoon diet jelly
> 1 tablespoon diet margarine
> 1 tablespoon diet mayonnaise
> 1 tablespoon diet Italian salad dressing

DAIRY FOODS

> ½ cup skim milk (no fat)
> 1 ounce Lite-line cheese
> ⅓ cup 1 percent fat cottage cheese
> ⅓ cup plain low-fat yogurt
> 1 ounce skim-milk mozzarella cheese

VEGETABLES

> 1 cup broccoli, raw or cooked
> 1 cup cabbage, red, raw or cooked
> 1 large carrot
> 1 cup parsley
> 1 cup pepper, green, or 1 whole pepper
> ½ serving any Super Salad

Lunch Menus

1 bagel spread with the following mixture:

⅓ cup 1 percent fat cottage cheese
1 green pepper, chopped
1 ounce parsley, chopped
1 scallion, chopped (optional)
¼ cucumber, chopped
1 tablespoon diet Italian salad dressing *or*
   Worcestershire sauce
fresh dill and pepper

If you prefer, you may substitute a 6-inch-diameter
Syrian bread pocket for the bagel.

Eat with:

1 small orange *or* ⅓ medium-sized cantaloupe

---

2 slices whole-wheat or rye bread *or* 1 6-inch-
   diameter whole-wheat Syrian bread pocket
1 4½-ounce can shrimp or 3½-ounce can
   water-packed tuna
1 green pepper, chopped
1 ounce parsley, chopped
1 scallion (optional)
1 tablespoon diet mayonnaise
1 teaspoon catsup, lemon juice, or Worcestershire sauce (optional)

Eat with:

½ cup skim milk

---

1 6-inch-diameter whole-wheat Syrian bread
pocket *or* 1 toasted English muffin
2 ounces skim-milk mozzarella cheese *or*
1½ slices Münster cheese
alfalfa sprouts — as much as you want
½ cucumber, thinly sliced (optional)

Eat with:

½ cup skim milk

---

2 matzos
1 ounce skim-milk mozzarella cheese *or*
2 tablespoons cheese spread

Eat with:

½ green pepper
1 carrot

---

1 cup plain low-fat yogurt mixed with:
½ sliced 6-inch-long banana *or* ¾ cup strawberries
2 teaspoons diet strawberry jam
2 tablespoons wheat germ

Eat with:

2 rice cakes *or* 4 Melba toast slices

1 large bran muffin

1 cup plain low-fat yogurt mixed with 2 teaspoons diet jelly

1 small orange *or* ½ grapefruit *or* ¾ cup strawberries

---

2 taco shells stuffed with:

1 3½-ounce can chili con carne with beans

2 ounces parsley, chopped (do not omit)

½ green pepper, chopped

2 tablespoons onions, chopped (optional)

shredded lettuce — as much as you want

hot sauce, salsa, chili peppers, chili powder, or garlic, to taste

---

1 6-inch-diameter Syrian bread pocket, split and toasted

2 ounces Fritos Bean Dip, mixed with onions, hot sauce, salsa, chili pepper, or any other seasoning

alfalfa sprouts, shredded lettuce, or cucumber (optional)

Eat with:

1 green pepper

1 carrot

---

1 bulkie roll *or* 2 slices rye bread *or* 2 slices whole-wheat bread

2 ounces spreadable sandwich meat (chicken salad, ham salad, tuna salad)

Eat with:

> 1 dill pickle (optional)
> 1 green pepper
> ½ cup skim milk

Cold Rice Salad made with:

⅔ cup leftover cold rice
2 ounces water-packed tuna
1 tablespoon diet Italian salad dressing
1 ounce parsley, chopped
1 carrot, chopped
scallions, chopped (optional)
thyme, oregano, to taste

Eat with:

> ½ cup skim milk

Dinner Exchange List

Choose *one* food from each of the categories listed below, or follow the dinner menu plans. Black coffee or tea or diet beverages as desired.

PROTEIN-RICH FOODS

(Unless otherwise stated, all weights are raw weight.)

FISH

3 ounces carp

3 ounces cod

3½ ounces haddock

2½ ounces halibut

3 ounces pike

2½ ounces pollock

3½ ounces salmon

2½ ounces smelts

2½ ounces sole

3½ ounces squid

2½ ounces swordfish

3 ounces striped bass

2 ounces water-packed tuna fish

SHELLFISH

1½ ounces clams, canned, drained

4 ounces clams, fresh

3 ounces crabmeat, canned

½ cup (3¾ ounces) lobster meat, cooked

3 ounces shrimp

MEAT AND POULTRY

1½ ounces very lean beef, cooked (approximately 2 ounces raw weight)

1½ ounces veal, cooked (approximately 2 ounces raw weight)

1½ ounces chicken or turkey (white meat only, no skin)

2½ ounces beef or chicken liver

CHEESE
½ cup 1 percent fat cottage cheese

SUPER SALAD

1 serving (or eat ½ serving at dinner and
    ½ serving at lunch)

DAIRY FOODS

½ cup skim milk (no fat)
1 ounce Lite-line cheese
½ ounce skim-milk mozzarella cheese
⅓ cup 1 percent fat cottage cheese
⅓ cup plain low-fat yogurt

BREAD AND OTHER STARCHY FOODS

2 slices whole-wheat, rye, or multigrain bread
1 6-inch-diameter Syrian bread pocket
1 cup rice, cooked
1 cup pasta, cooked
1 cup potato, mashed
2 medium-sized potatoes, baked

VEGETABLES
(Unless otherwise stated, measurements are for
cooked vegetables.)

1 cup (4 ounces) asparagus
1 cup beans, green
1 cup beans, wax

½ cup beets
1 cup broccoli
⅔ cup Brussels sprouts
½ cup cabbage, red
1 cup cabbage, regular, cooked or raw
1 cup or 1 large raw carrot
1 cup cauliflower
¾ cup collard, dandelion, or beet greens
¾ cup kale
1 cup lettuce, romaine (add to salad if desired)
1 large pepper, green
1 cup spinach
1 cup squash, summer (yellow) or zucchini
  (green)
1 cup tomatoes, stewed

FRUIT

2 medium-sized fresh apricots
3 medium-sized apricots, canned in water
½ cup blueberries
¼ cantaloupe, 5-inch diameter
½ medium-sized grapefruit
½ cup grapefruit segments, canned, packed
  in water
¼ honeydew melon, 5-inch diameter
1 large nectarine
1 small 2-inch-diameter orange or ½ cup
  orange sections

1 medium-sized peach
½ cup pineapple, raw
2 medium-sized purple plums, canned,
  packed in water
¾ cup or 10 large strawberries
1 medium-sized tangelo
2 small tangerines
¾ cup watermelon

Dinner Menus

PASTA I

2 ounces Superoni shells or spaghetti, broken
  into pieces
1 zucchini, sliced
1 onion
1 clove garlic, crushed, to taste
1 teaspoon cooking oil
1 cup tomatoes, canned, crushed or puréed
10 mushrooms
oregano, basil, crushed red pepper, salt,
  pepper

Cook Superoni according to package directions and
drain. Sauté zucchini, onion, and garlic in cooking
oil. Mix remaining ingredients and cook for 5 minutes. Pour in cooked Superoni, blend well, and heat
through. Instead of making sauce from scratch, you
can substitute ½ can of zucchini in tomato sauce
and add mushrooms and onions if desired.

Eat with:

    1 serving any Super Salad

PASTA II

This recipe takes some time. Cook cauliflower and cheese sauce ahead, if possible, to save time.

    2 ounces Superoni shells or spaghetti, broken into pieces

    1 10-ounce box cauliflower, frozen, or 1½ cups cauliflower, fresh, cooked

    ½ cup 1 percent fat cottage cheese

    ½ ounce skim-milk mozzarella cheese, shredded, chopped, or grated

    curry, mustard, fresh nutmeg, fresh dill, Worcestershire sauce, chili powder, to taste

Cook Superoni according to package directions, drain, and set aside. Cook cauliflower and drain. Add the cottage cheese and shredded cheese to the drained cauliflower and heat for 5 to 10 minutes or until cheese is melted. Add the spices and Superoni. Cook all together on top of stove for 10 minutes.

Eat with:

    ½ portion any Super Salad

PASTA III

    2 ounces Superoni spaghetti, broken into
      pieces
    ½ onion, chopped
    2 cloves garlic, crushed
    1 teaspoon cooking oil
    1½ cups canned meatless spaghetti sauce
    4 ounces mushrooms, fresh, canned, or frozen
    oregano, basil, fennel, rosemary, to taste
    dash of wine (optional)

Cook Superoni according to package directions and
drain. Sauté onion and garlic in cooking oil. Add
the remaining ingredients and cook for 5 minutes.
Mix with Superoni and heat through.

Eat with:

    ½ portion any Super Salad

MACARONI SALAD

    ½ cup macaroni, dry
    ¼ cup tuna fish, water-packed, *or* leftover
      chicken *or* turkey *or* lean ham
    ½ cup celery
    1 tablespoon onions or 1 scallion, chopped
    1 dill pickle, chopped, or fresh dill (optional)
    1 tablespoon diet mayonnaise

Cook macaroni, drain, and cool. Mix all the ingredients together.

Eat with:
    1 serving any Super Salad

RICE SALAD
    ½ cup rice, dry
    1 cup broth *or* bouillon
    1 tablespoon diet mayonnaise *or* diet Italian
      salad dressing
    1 stalk celery, chopped
    1 scallion, chopped
    1 ounce chicken *or* turkey *or* ham, cooked
    2 tablespoons parsley, chopped
    1 small carrot, chopped
    thyme or rosemary, oregano, basil, salt,

Cook rice in broth or bouillon; cool. Mix the remaining ingredients with the rice. Serve cold.

Eat with:
    ½ cup skim milk

POTATO SALAD
    2 medium potatoes
    1 egg, hard-boiled, chopped
    1 ounce lean ham *or* cold chicken *or* cold turkey
    1 tablespoon (1 ounce or more) parsley,
      chopped
    1 tablespoon diet mayonnaise
    scallion or onion (optional)
    thyme, oregano, basil, salt, pepper, to taste

Boil the potatoes. When they are cool, peel and chop them. Mix in the remaining ingredients.

Eat with:

> 1 serving any Super Salad

POTATO BOATS

> 1 large potato, baking
> 1 ounce hard cheese, meltable, chopped
> 1 ounce lean ham *or* chicken *or* turkey, chopped
> 2 tablespoons parsley, chopped
> 1 tablespoon diet margarine
> salt, pepper

Bake potato until it is done. Split, remove the inside, and mix with cheese and all other ingredients except parsley; then fill potato skins. Put back in oven and bake until cheese is melted. Sprinkle parsley on top.

Eat with:

> 1 serving any Super Salad

RICE AND MEAT SAUCE

> ½ cup rice, dry
> 1 cup broth *or* bouillon
> 1½ ounces lean hamburger, raw
> 1 onion, chopped

1 green pepper, chopped (if you don't like
cooked pepper, add it to salad instead)
1 clove garlic
1 cup tomato juice
¼ cup mushrooms, sliced, chopped, or whole
oregano, basil, crushed red pepper, fennel,
salt, pepper
1 tablespoon parsley

Cook rice in broth or bouillon. Brown hamburger in
heavy nonstick skillet. Add onion, green pepper,
garlic, tomato juice, mushrooms, and seasonings.
Stir in rice. Sprinkle parsley on top. Cover and cook
for 10 minutes.

Eat with:

½ serving any Super Salad

CHINESE-STYLE MEAT AND BROCCOLI

6 ounces broccoli, raw, peeled and cut into
slices
1 teaspoon cooking oil, preferably sesame
seed oil
1 ounce lean meat (beef *or* turkey *or*
chicken), cooked, cut into pieces
1 tablespoon soy sauce
1 clove garlic
1 teaspoon fresh ginger

Stir-fry broccoli slices in oil in a heavy pan until
stalks turn greener. Add meat and seasonings. Cook
until warm. (To "heat up" sauce try adding 1 tea-

spoon chili bean paste or a few drops Tabasco sauce.)

Eat with:

> 1 cup cooked rice
> 1 serving any Super Salad

One-Pot Meals

MEAT, VEGETABLES, AND RICE

> 1 cup rice, cooked
> 1 cup vegetable chow mein, canned, drained
> 1 ounce chicken *or* turkey, cooked
> soy sauce and garlic powder

Warm ingredients in a saucepan on top of the stove and serve.

Eat with:

> 1 cup skim milk

CLAM AND OYSTER STEW

> ½ cup canned clams, drained
> ½ 10-ounce can oyster stew
> 1 1-pound can potatoes, drained

Mix all the ingredients together and heat for 10 minutes.

Eat with:

> 1 serving any Super Salad

SHRIMP CREOLE

> ½ 3½-ounce can shrimp
> ½ 10-ounce can Creole sauce
> 2 waffle squares, frozen

Mix shrimp and Creole sauce together, cook over medium heat for 5 minutes, and pour on toasted waffle squares. (You can substitute 1½ ounces of cooked chicken *or* turkey *or* water-packed tuna for shrimp.)

Eat with:

> 1 serving any Super Salad

SOUP WITH PASTA OR RICE

> 1 cup Chunky Beef with Country Vegetables soup
> 1 cup rice or pasta, cooked

Mix soup with rice or pasta, heat, and serve.

Eat with:

> 1 serving any Super Salad

CHILI CON CARNE WITH BEANS

> 1 5-ounce can chili con carne with beans
> 3½ ounces kidney beans, canned
> any chili seasoning to taste

Heat ingredients together and serve.

Eat with:

>   1 serving any Super Salad
>   1 orange *or* ¾ cup strawberries

BEANS AND BEEF

>   1 ounce lean ground beef
>   1 tablespoon chili sauce or catsup
>   ½ 7-ounce can vegetarian baked beans in
>   tomato sauce

Cook beef in chili sauce, then blend in beans, heat, and serve.

Eat with:

>   1 serving any Super Salad

EGG AND SAUSAGE

>   2 Morningstar Farms breakfast links,
>   frozen
>   1 egg

Cook the sausage in a nonstick skillet. Push the sausage to one side and fry or scramble the egg.

Eat with:

>   1 English muffin *or* 2 frozen French toast
>   squares
>   ½ cup skim milk
>   1 serving any Super Salad

9

The Morning-After Diet

> "I can stay on the diet for about three
> and a half weeks. Then, unless I can eat
> what *I* want, not what the diet tells me,
> I self-destruct. So I plan a treat for my-
> self; I go out with friends and eat or
> drink whatever I like. And the next
> morning, I go right on the Morning-
> After Diet."
>
> — *A patient*

SOONER OR LATER, *everyone* on a diet is likely to
have a lapse, whether it is a carefully organized
one, like that of the patient quoted above, or
an impulsive accident, or simply one that can't be
helped. If everyone in the crowd wants to go out
for fried clams, chances are you'll go along and eat
them too. And although you certainly didn't intend
to eat the remains of your daughter's birthday cake,
somehow you just did. The sight of someone licking
a creamy ice-cream cone on a hot summer day will
probably make you look for the nearest ice-cream
store. And if you are invited to a superb French res-

taurant, you're not really going to order a grape-fruit and broiled fish, are you?

Of course not. We aren't machines that eat auto-matically. No warning bell goes off when our cal-orie limit is reached. And being on a diet, even this one that satisfies your carbohydrate craving, will not take away your susceptibility to fattening, mouth-watering foods.

So when the inevitable succumbing to tempta-tions occurs, and it will, do not despair. It is not a sin and you should not feel guilty. But what should you do? You should immediately go on the Morn-ing-After Diet.

The Morning-After Diet removes pounds quickly because it supplies only 800 calories a day. It can be followed for a day, to compensate for the ice-cream cone, or for as long as a week, to take care of larger transgressions. In one week on this diet, you should lose between 2 and 4 recently acquired pounds. When the week is over and you are back to your pre-overeating weight, go back on the Carbohy-drate Craver's Diet.

The rapid weight loss produced by the Morning-After Diet makes it a useful antidote to any overeating situation. It allows you to enjoy a culinary indulgence — perhaps a luxurious Sunday brunch or a night-long wedding feast — without worrying about what eating those extra calories will do to your weight-loss schedule. It is also useful in removing weight rapidly after a stress-induced eating binge. The last thing you should worry about when eating out of stress is what those extra calories will do to your diet. You have other things to worry about; otherwise you would not be overeating. When life is more bearable, go on the Morning-After Diet. It will make you feel in control of your eating once again, and the rapid weight loss that will occur will remove the guilt and anger that accompanied your overeating.

The Morning-After Diet should be followed *only* after overeating; it should never be used to accelerate weight loss. You may feel impatient with the slow, steady weight loss produced by the Carbohydrate Craver's Diet and think to yourself, "Boy, if I go on this diet, I will really be able to reach my goal, fast." You will — and then the lack of carbohydrate on the Morning-After Diet will also cause you to gain back the weight really fast as you start overeating carbohydrates again. (You went over this route many times in the past, remember?) The diet is an antidote for overeating, not a quick-weight-loss plan. Because there are no snacks on the Morning-After Diet, you should not follow it for more than seven days. You will become too carbohydrate hungry to make it tolerable if you stay on it longer.

A seven-day menu plan is given. You can follow the menus in any sequence or follow the same menu for as many days as you wish. You must, however, eat all the food on each day's meal plan. Do not eliminate anything or make any substitutions. The foods were chosen to make sure that all your nutrient needs are met. If you change any, you may be depriving yourself of some necessary vitamin or mineral.

Weigh yourself before starting the diet and then again three days later. If you are back to your pre-overeating weight, stop the diet; otherwise, continue until the end of the week.

And be sure to start the diet the morning after. Don't wait. You will be mildly angry at yourself for overeating, regardless of how much joy it gave you, so turn that anger into motivation for removing those extra pounds. If you walk around with them for too long, they may begin to feel comfortable and stay around forever.

THE MORNING-AFTER DIET

Unlimited amounts of black coffee or tea or diet beverages are allowed with each meal.

Day 1

Breakfast

> 1 cup (1 container) vanilla-flavored low-fat yogurt
> 1 tablespoon wheat germ

Lunch

3½ ounces (1 small can) water-packed tuna
½ serving any Super Salad
1 3-inch-diameter whole-wheat Syrian bread
  pocket

Dinner

2½ ounces (raw weight) lean steak *or* 3½
  ounces (raw weight) other cut of lean meat,
  broiled, braised, pot roasted, or stewed
⅔ cup carrots
½ serving any Super Salad
¾ cup strawberries *or* ½ grapefruit
1 cup skim milk

Day 2

Breakfast

1 small orange *or* ¾ cup strawberries
2 slices whole-wheat toast
2 teaspoons diet jelly
1 cup skim milk

Lunch

2 ounces sliced turkey *or* chicken

1 tablespoon diet mayonnaise *or* catsup *or* mustard

½ serving any Super Salad

1 3-inch-diameter whole-wheat Syrian bread pocket

Dinner

3½ ounces broiled or baked haddock or similar white fish

⅔ cup cooked broccoli

½ serving any Super Salad

1 cup skim milk

Day 3

Breakfast

1 egg, any style (use nonstick pan if scrambling or frying)

2 squares frozen waffles *or* 1 English muffin

1 tablespoon diet syrup

Lunch

1 cup (1 container) vanilla-, coffee-, or lemon-flavored low-fat yogurt

1 tablespoon wheat germ
½ serving any Super Salad

Dinner

3½ ounces baked chicken without skin
⅔ cup cooked Brussels sprouts *or* kale *or* mustard *or* turnip greens, fresh or frozen
½ serving any Super Salad
1 cup skim milk

Day 4

Breakfast

1 bagel, regular size
1 tablespoon diet grape jelly
1 cup skim milk

Lunch

⅔ cup 1 percent fat cottage cheese
1 tablespoon wheat germ
½ green pepper, chopped
1 ounce or more parsley, chopped
1 cucumber, chopped
1 teaspoon Worcestershire sauce
scallions, chopped (optional)
few drops hot sauce (optional)

Mix all the ingredients together.

> 1 small banana (6 inches long)

Dinner

> 5 ounces (raw weight) baked or broiled shrimp *or* 4 ounces halibut *or* other white fish
> ½ cup green beans, cooked or raw
> 1 serving any Super Salad
> ½ cup skim milk

Day 5

Breakfast

> ⅓ medium-sized cantaloupe *or* ½ grapefruit
> 2-egg omelet, cooked in nonstick pan
> 1 cup skim milk

Lunch

> 1 3-inch-diameter whole-wheat Syrian bread pocket stuffed with:
> 2 ounces cooked chicken (canned, left over from menu Day 3, or bought at deli counter)
> ½ serving any Super Salad
> 1 tablespoon diet mayonnaise
> mustard *or* catsup (optional)
> alfalfa sprouts (optional)

Dinner

4 ounces (raw weight) lean hamburger,
  broiled or pan fried
1 cup cooked spinach
½ serving any Super Salad
1 cup skim milk

Day 6

Breakfast

1 cup fortified cereal (from list on pages
  81–82)
¾ cup strawberries *or* 1 small orange *or*
  ½ small banana
1 cup skim milk

Lunch

Greek Salad made with:
2 ounces parsley
2 ounces feta cheese
⅙ head lettuce
1 tomato
1 green pepper
1 cucumber
1 scallion
1 ounce alfalfa sprouts
1 hard-boiled egg
2 tablespoons diet Italian salad dressing

Dinner

6 broiled scallops (8 ounces raw weight) *or* 5 ounces
  herring in wine sauce, drained
⅔ cup cooked mushrooms (boiled or steamed)
1 serving any Super Salad

Day 7

Breakfast

⅔ cup Bran Chex cereal
1 cup skim milk

Lunch

2 ounces lean ham *or* 2 ounces water-packed
  tuna, chopped, added to ½ serving any
  Super Salad
celery, cucumber, scallions (optional)
1 tablespoon diet mayonnaise
1 3-inch-diameter whole-wheat Syrian bread
  pocket

Dinner

6 ounces (raw weight) baked filet of sole *or*
  other white fish
1 cup cooked cauliflower
½ serving any Super Salad
1 cup skim milk

10

The Premenstrual Sweet Tooth

"It's ridiculous. Every day I walk past a candy store on the way home from work and never even notice that it's there. But right before my period, I find myself inside the store, buying a gigantic candy bar."
— *Editor of a woman's magazine*

FOR A FEW DAYS every month, many women, especially if they are carbohydrate cravers anyway, find themselves with an intense hunger for carbohydrates. Often without even realizing what is happening, they feel an uncontrollable urge to eat sweets.

If you are one whose premenstrual symptoms include an insatiable need for sweet carbohydrates, you know how miserable it is to fight the urge. But why fight it? Why not give in and eat the sweets?

Because, I hear you saying, a diet of only sweets is unhealthy and it's fattening.

141

All true — but I'm talking about only a few days, at the most, in a month. You won't die of malnutrition — you've been eating a very healthy diet the rest of the month. To combat the fattening part, I propose a diet of sweets that doesn't exceed 1100 calories a day. You won't gain weight on that, I promise you.

Here's how to go about it.

Mark on your calendar the days when you are likely to develop your craving for sweets. And before those days arrive, make a menu plan: It might consist of a large Mars bar for breakfast, two jelly doughnuts for lunch, an ice-cream sandwich for a midafternoon snack, and six Oreos, one brownie, and a soft ice-cream cone for dinner. Look up the calories of the foods you plan to eat and make sure they don't exceed your caloric limit. Keep the "menu" handy, but don't actually buy the foods until you need them. No point straining your will power.

How will you know when the Sweet-Tooth Day arrives? You usually can tell because you wake up feeling slightly out of sorts, have more than the usual trouble getting through routine activities, feel less able to cope with the normal daily irritants, and, above all, seem to have an insatiable need to eat carbohydrates. Look at your calendar, and if you are premenstrual, go to your menu plan for those days and start eating.

You may actually find that as your stomach fills up with sweets, your disposition is also sweetening. Serotonin levels in the brain increase after any carbohydrate is eaten, and among the feelings serotonin controls are relaxation, calmness, and tranquillity. So not only are you being nice to yourself by eating chocolate on those days, you end up being nicer to others as well.

You may not always know when your premenstrual sweet tooth is about to attack, or it may come at some inconvenient time when you can't get out of the house. Sometimes you may find yourself needing to eat something sweet late at night.

As one of my patients related, "It was Sunday night and I just felt funny. I couldn't sit still. I kept looking for something sweet to eat, which was a joke because I never have anything in the house. Finally, I was so desperate that I made myself a cup of tea and put about three tablespoons of sugar in it. Normally, I hate sweetened tea. But it was exactly what I needed. I felt calm after I drank it and left the kitchen. Wouldn't you know, the next day I woke up with my period."

If you are caught unprepared for an onslaught of a sweet tooth, do what this patient did. Drink something hot with 2 to 3 tablespoons of sugar dissolved in it or put the same amount of jam or jelly on crackers. Both methods will satisfy your urge to eat sweets.

Don't worry that all this sugar consumption is going to damage your diet or your health. You are going to indulge in this type of eating no more often than one or two days a month, and as long as you brush your teeth (to prevent cavities) and limit yourself to 1100 calories, nothing will be damaged but your bad disposition.

11

Eating Your Way Through Stress

STRESS IS the most common cause of overeating and the most serious threat to a diet. Although some (lucky!) people respond to stress by losing their appetite, in my experience most people, and especially carbohydrate cravers, overeat instead.

In general, two types of eating are done in response to stress. When the stress is acute but short-lived, the eating is usually intense and also brief. The foods eaten tend to be very high in calories, often very sweet, and pleasure the taste buds as well as comforting the eater. The eater feels better for having eaten the food — unless guilt rears its annoying head. The following example of eating in the middle of a brief stressful period is typical.

"I was distraught. It was late in the afternoon and I hadn't found a folding table for my husband's birthday dinner party. Where was I going to seat those ten extra guests? I had been crisscrossing the highway from one shopping center to the other, and every store I went into had either nothing or nothing appropriate. As I was leaving the fifth large department store, almost in tears, I saw at the check-out counter a stack of those gooey, chocolate-covered candy bars. I had to have one even though normally they are too sweet for me. I bought it, tore open the wrapper, and practically finished it by the time I reached the car. And ten minutes later, as I was heading for the next shopping center, I no longer really cared whether I found a table or not. I was figuring out where on the floor people could sit."

Often the stressful situation is prolonged, lasting several hours or even for a few days. Waiting for a critical phone call, or for your teenager to return from his first night out with the car, or working on a tedious and overdue report are examples of a chronic stress. The intensity of the stress is less than the example I described above, and so is the eating. People usually respond by constant nibbling. As long as the stress continues, the hand continues to deliver food to the mouth.

An editor told me that the only way she can get through rewriting difficult manuscripts is to eat continually.

"I am really disgusted with myself because I'll never lose any weight. In fact, I had agreed to go on a diet with a friend, and we told each other that we would start last Sunday. But last Sunday, I was sitting at my desk with a box of wheat crackers, eating them with one hand and writing with the other. She called up to find out how I was doing on the diet just as I had stuffed another cracker into my mouth. I had to tell her, through a mouthful of cracker crumbs, that the diet was off, at least until I finished editing the book."

Obviously, these eating episodes do not promote the cause of weight loss. And knowledge that one is smothering the diet with cookies doesn't help the stress either. Looking at a bulging stomach after the stress has passed is somewhat less than comforting, even if the eating helped you get through the crisis.

The problem, as you are probably aware, is that when you are in the middle of something unpleasant, you are in no mood to discipline yourself. If you want that piece of chocolate cake, you are not going to eat a piece of cauliflower instead! And you know as you reach for that second piece of chocolate cake that the diet is ruined, but you simply don't care — and then you often become so angry at yourself for not caring that you tell yourself you might as well "pig out" anyway. The diet is lost, your figure is lost, so why not eat?

A schoolteacher patient of mine said, "I know that it isn't the first dish of ice cream that destroys me. Rationally I realize that my diet can absorb those extra calories. But I can't shake that feeling of guilt and self-hatred that comes when I've done something like that. So after eating the first dish, I tell myself that I might as well eat the half gallon. What difference does it make anyway? I figure that I will never be able to control my eating, so I might as well go ahead and eat."

The dieter is left with a dilemma: He knows that under some circumstances eating is the only way he can cope with stress, but he also knows that eating will prevent him from losing weight. What is the solution?

The solution is to eat when no other response is possible and to eat in such a way that maximum relief and minimum damage occur. Here's how.

Acute stresses — such as those felt by the woman who couldn't find a table for her husband's birthday party — call for consumption of a "coping food." A coping food should contain substantial amounts of carbohydrate (like the ones on your snack list) but also should provide enormous amounts of pleasure. If possible, the food should be one which you absolutely adore eating but have avoided totally on the diet because it is too fattening. It is a food of which fantasies are made. If your mouth waters at the thought of eating a seventeen-layer chocolate cake, or a honey-drenched piece of baklava, or a mound of whipped-cream-covered strawberries on a freshly baked shortcake, or a piece of hot bread drenched with butter, then these foods are good coping foods. Of course, it is usually not possible to obtain that fantasy food, especially in the middle of a crisis. But the food you do choose should be as pleasurable and self-indulging as possible. You will know you are eating the right food because you will be saying to yourself as you reach for it, "I want to eat *that* now and I don't care how fattening it is."

But how can eating the food diminish your feelings of stress? It works because the carbohydrate in the food, as you know already, will promote the manufacture of serotonin. Serotonin is involved in other behaviors in addition to regulating carbohydrate hunger. It is one of the brain chemicals that puts you to sleep at night, and there is already some evidence that it makes people feel relaxed. In fact, you may have been aware of this change in your emotional state after you have had your carbohydrate snack.

A nurse who is a typical carbohydrate craver told me, "I really think of myself as a nice person and am usually very good-natured. But right before I eat my carbohydrate snack, I am grumpy and irritable. And afterward, I am back to my normal, placid self."

So when you are upset, tense, anxious, nervous, or frustrated, eating carbohydrate will calm you down and make it easier to cope with the stress that is producing these unpleasant emotions.

However, in order for the coping food to work most effectively, you must eat it in as relaxed and tranquil an environment as possible. Don't grab the snack, throw it into your mouth, and gulp it down the way a seal eats a fish. Even though the calming effect of serotonin will still occur, it may be submerged by your rather frenzied eating (and probably by your emerging guilt). If possible, refrain from eating the food until you have found a quiet place in which to do so. Take ten minutes to sit down, put your feet up, and enjoy your food. If the weather is nice, sit outside. If you are away from home, find a pleasant restaurant and sit down so you can watch people on the street go by, or take a newspaper or magazine with you to prolong your respite.

Eat slowly, leisurely, savoring every bit.

This unhurried, calm consumption of the coping food will reinforce the effects of eating the carbohydrate itself. After twenty minutes or so, you really will feel better. The cause of the stress will not have vanished, but your ability to deal with it will be increased.

Don't feel guilty about what you have just eaten. That will destroy this lovely feeling of relaxation and tranquillity. There is no reason to feel guilty. Regardless of how large the piece of cake or how many scoops of ice cream in that sundae, you can always get rid of the weight quickly. After the stress has passed and you can resume your normal routine, go on the Morning-After Diet. In three or four days at the most, your extra pounds from eating the coping food will have disappeared.

Think of the coping food as an edible tranquilizer. It produces the same relaxing effect as other tranquilizing agents but, unlike those, causes no lasting damage. Unfortunately for all of us who prefer a piece of pie rather than a glass of bourbon during stress, society has not romanticized this way of dealing with crises. As you know, it is very common in the movies or television for a person, in crisis, to be given a shot glass full of whiskey and told, "Here, drink this, you'll feel better." He drinks it, says, "Boy, that's what I needed," and goes out and slays the monster. Have you ever seen the hero handed a plate filled with freshly baked biscuits or warm apple pie and told, "Here, eat this, you'll feel better"? Of course not. So even though eating is incomparably safer (for you and society) than drinking during stress, it is not yet a socially favored behavior. Don't let this bother you. You know what works to make you feel better, and you can take comfort in your eating by realizing that no one has ever been arrested for driving under the influence of a chocolate bar.

Once you have eaten the coping food, stop. Don't have another portion. One serving is enough and should not lead to unrestrained gobbling. If you were drinking a cocktail or taking a tranquilizer to calm you down, you would not go ahead and consume a quart of gin or a bottle of Valium. The coping food is also a tranquilizer — take only as directed, and do not overdose.

Continuing to eat even though you are feeling more relaxed is a symptom of underlying problems with your relationship with food (and perhaps with people who want you to lose weight). If you are vulnerable to stress-induced *binging,* then seek help. It is too difficult a problem to solve alone.

Chronic mild stress that persists for hours or even a day or two calls for another type of eating: continuous nibbling on low-calorie finger foods. This stress is alleviated not so much by the actual swallowing of the food but by the act of putting something into the mouth, over and over again. Touching the mouth with the fingers seems to be very soothing under such types of stress and you may already be aware of doing this when you must get through a long period of tension or worry. The editor mentioned earlier was very sensitive to her need to nibble on foods that engaged the fingers and the lips, and when she ran out of crackers or carrot sticks she felt as bereft as an infant whose pacifier drops to the floor.

The one problem with this type of nibbling is that you do end up swallowing the food, and the food ends up contributing calories and pounds.

Since it is unlikely that chewing crushed ice (a zero-calorie food) will satisfy you, it is necessary to find other foods with as low a calorie count as possible and as high a finger-to-mouth contact as possible.

All vegetables that are high in water are good nibbling foods: Some examples are celery, dill pickles, cucumber, radishes, mushrooms, sauerkraut, string beans, cabbage, alfalfa sprouts, baked potato skins, green and yellow summer squash, and cauliflower. If your stomach can endure no more of these high-fiber, low-calorie vegetables and cries out for more soothing textured foods, consider some starchy low-fat items: pretzels, Melba toast, rice cakes, puffed rice or wheat, popcorn, cold cooked rice or elbow macaroni, and Grape-nuts cereal.

Break or cut all large pieces of the nibbling food into bite-sized portions. Break the pretzels, string beans, cabbage, and cauliflower into tiny pieces, crumble the Melba toast and rice cakes, and dice the pickles, cucumbers, and squash.

Eat everything with your fingers. Everything.

How can you possibly eat something like cold rice or Grape-nuts with your fingers? You can, one granule after the other. Ah, but you say it will take a long time to eat it that way, that it is messy, that rice will be stuck all over your chin or your paper will be littered with Grape-nuts. True. And putting those tidbits into your mouth and wiping your chin and picking up the Grape-nuts from the paper will be wonderfully distracting. You will end up eating very little because it takes so much time and effort to eat this way. Remember, the idea is to engage in sustained finger-to-mouth activity, not consumatory (that is, eating) activity. Eating with your fingers fulfills this objective extremely well.

Control the amount of food you will be nibbling on by preparing a large volume at once, making sure it is in the proper size, and then taking it with you in a bowl or wheelbarrow to where you are working or waiting. Don't go back into the kitchen. This is what you will be eating, so try to make it last several hours.

A patient told me that this method prevented her from wandering into the kitchen every time she wanted a break and eating anything her eyes noticed. "Before, I ate leftovers, peanuts, candy, cheese, cold cuts, cottage cheese, crackers, cookies, potato chips — you name it. But now I pretend the kitchen doesn't exist. When I want to put something into my mouth, I just dip into my nibbling bowl."

Some of you may find that sucking rather than nibbling is more comforting during periods of long-term stress. If this is the case, suck on lollipops, popsicles, or homemade frozen cubes of diet soda or tea or coffee. Stick a wooden stick into the ice cube so you can remove it from your mouth to talk. Also try using a straw for drinking; the sipping is very comforting.

Even with these low-calorie nibbling or sucking foods, you may be consuming many more calories than you should on the diet. Since you don't want to worry about gaining weight while you are dealing with your other worries, you should try to cut back on the foods you eat during other times of the day. Consider skipping a meal that follows a prolonged period of nibbling. Your stomach is probably quite full, and you may be eating the meal simply as a distraction or social event. It is doubtful that you are hungry. Sit at the table but don't eat. You can also skip your snack, especially if you have been snacking on a lot of high-carbohydrate foods. However, if your nibbling foods have been mainly vegetables, do eat your snack. As soon as this self-limiting stressful situation passes, go on the Morning-After Diet for at least two or three days.

I have been talking about infrequent periods of overeating caused by stress; clearly, if your life contains many predictable and routine difficulties that make you want to eat, dieting is not going to be successful. Eating a coping food or nibbling cannot be done often. These responses must be used only during acute and rare periods of emotional turmoil or frustrating work situations. But if you have to turn in a report every Friday or if the neighbor's dog overturns your garbage can every

Tuesday, you cannot use these methods to deal with such weekly problems. You will never lose weight.

There are bookshelves filled with manuals on how to reduce stress and even workshops on stress management. Sometimes the techniques are worth knowing; many of them are based on common sense and experience. However, I have found that my patients who have memorized these manuals never could follow their instructions once in the middle of a stressful situation and always ate instead.

As one woman told me, "I knew all the methods all right. As soon as my mother hung up, I started in. First the book, then the needlepoint, then I washed my hair, ironed some clothes, called a friend. And then, I ate. These techniques simply pushed back the inevitable."

Although you may find ways of avoiding food when you are upset, if the suggested methods don't work for you either, don't be discouraged. It may be better to expend your energy in avoiding or preventing recurrent stressful situations than practicing ways of not eating during them.

What you must do first is to identify these stressful triggers to eating. Some of them may be very obvious, such as fighting rush-hour traffic every night or contending with screaming preschoolers every winter afternoon. Think of ways in which you can remove yourself from the stressful situation.

For example, one of my patients used to consume

a box of Wheat Thins every afternoon between four and five while her kids were tearing up the living room. She finally decided to ask a teenager to baby-sit at that time and took herself off to the library. She stopped eating (no food or drink allowed in the library), and felt that she was in control again.

Another patient, who was recently divorced, saved his household tasks for Sundays and then became very angry at having to stay inside and do them. He would leave the house, go to a nearby grocery store, buy and consume two large cakes. I persuaded him to do his laundry during the week and to join a hiking club so he had company over the weekend. His cake eating stopped totally.

While you are in the middle of a stressful situation, you are unlikely to stop eating and say to yourself, "Why am I doing this?" But after the episode has passed and you can analyze the causes somewhat objectively, don't ask yourself why you overate; rather, ask yourself what you can do to prevent it the next time. Sometimes the solutions are not easy, as with the patient whose eating was always triggered by the inevitable weekly phone call from her mother. She wasn't about to move to another continent, and she couldn't tell her mother to stop calling. She actually sought professional psychological help to work out her rather complex relationship to her mother and eating. However, talking over your problems with friends or relatives usually will be sufficient to suggest some workable solutions.

Another common cause of stress-related eating is using food as a way of procrastinating or diverting oneself from an unpleasant task. For example, you say to yourself that you will attack that basket of ironing as soon as you finish the snack. Soon one snack leads to another, and all the snacks are finished before the laundry is started.

Or eating is used as a break from a tedious, unpleasant, or exhausting bout of work. A doctor told me that when he was an intern, the supper served at midnight was the most important meal of the day. "We were never that hungry, but going to the cafeteria gave us a chance to get off the wards, sit down, and talk for a few minutes. I must have gained thirty-five pounds that year because unless you were eating, you had no excuse for staying in the cafeteria."

If you are one of the many who tend to use eating to procrastinate or divert, you can, of course, alter this trait, do everything on time, and never stop working until you are finished. However, until you accomplish this near-impossible change of personality, try finding other pleasurable diversions or ways of procrastinating. A friend of mine always has a good mystery novel in the house when she does some unpleasant type of writing. She portions out the chapters to herself: one before starting, and one after writing so many pages. Since she is always eager to find out "who did it," she works hard and goes immediately to the book, rather than to the cookies, when she takes her breaks.

Finally, if life is particularly stressful, consider halting the Carbohydrate Craver's Diet until the crisis has passed. Disciplining yourself into following a diet is not easy, especially if your mind is occupied by many urgent problems. Try to maintain the weight loss you have produced already, and when life settles down into a more placid routine, start again on the diet.

12

Lead Me Not into Temptation

LOSING WEIGHT wouldn't be nearly so hard if you could go off somewhere and escape all the major and minor stimuli that make you eat too much. That's why it is so easy to lose weight at those health spas, where the only thing you have to worry about is whether to have your hair done before or after your massage. Unfortunately for most of the dieters of the world, it is necessary to continue on with the rest of life while dieting, and often one interferes with the other.

Any number of tempting eating situations confront the dieter: eating out socially at someone's home or at a restaurant, business meals, travel, vacation, relatives who want to overfeed you, friends whose pride in their cooking is stronger than their support for your diet. Unfortunately, becoming a hermit doesn't solve anything (although hermits are usually skinny), and you have to find solutions for these tempting situations. They will pop up again after you have finished the Carbohydrate Craver's Diet, and it is better to work out solutions now when, if you fail, the only consequence is failure to lose weight as fast as you would like. If you give in to these temptations after the diet is over, you risk adding some pounds on to your newly acquired thin figure.

Social Dining

Dieting at the home of friends or acquaintances is a delicate situation. Obviously, you can't offend your hostess by refusing to eat a dish that required five hours of preparation. But you don't want to undo a week's worth of dieting. And part of you really wants to eat that chocolate cake.

The first thing you must do is make up your mind: Are you going to stick with the diet or not? If you decide you really want to eat all the food at the dinner and forget the calories, then do so, and prepare to go on the Morning-After Diet the next day. But make the decision consciously so that you don't eat because you gave in to pressure or to your own lack of will power.

Second, if you are going to abide by the Carbohydrate Craver's Diet, take your hostess aside before the meal begins and indicate that you will not be able to eat everything she will be serving. Tell it to her privately so you won't have to make a public announcement. Now — and this is very important — tell her the reason you must eat with restraint is that you are on a *low-fat diet*. Do not breathe a word about losing weight. Of course you know that a low-fat diet must be a low-calorie diet, since it is fat that really adds the calories to food. But you don't have to explain this. Just say that your doctor thought it would be good for your health to cut back on fat and so you are avoiding all high-fat foods like red meat (except the lean varieties), cream, eggs, butter, cheese. Tell her that you will eat what you can and would appreciate it if she wouldn't mention anything to the other guests because you don't want them to feel uncomfortable.

This reason for eating lightly at a dinner party is perfect. If you tell the hostess that you are on a reducing diet, you might have to play the "let's see if we can get the dieter to eat fattening food" game. Or be subjected to a long discussion of whether you have to lose weight or not. But no one can quarrel with a desire to eat a healthy diet, especially if the unspoken reason for doing so involves the possibility of developing heart disease. No one wants to promote heart attacks.

What can you eat after such an announcement? Diet-sized portions of poultry, fish, veal, lamb, potatoes, rice or other grains, salad, vegetables, and fruit for dessert. If little is available that satisfies your diet needs, eat enough of what you can to take the edge off your hunger and wait until you get home to eat dinner. If, by the way, someone comments on your decreasing size, mention that your doctor said that a side effect of this low-fat diet is weight loss.

Restaurant Dining

Eating in restaurants is better and worse than eating in someone else's home. Better because you decide what to eat; worse because there are so many tempting foods to eat. Avoid eating in restaurants where it is impossible to select low-calorie foods: pizza and sub shops, fried-seafood and fast-food restaurants, street stalls.

Here is a brief guide to what to eat in restaurants. If you can call ahead and learn the volume or weight of the portions they serve, you will be even better prepared to "eat thin" when eating out.

Chinese: Eat vegetable, bean curd, or vegetable and poultry or fish dishes; dishes featuring shredded meat and vegetables wrapped in thin pancakes; soups; ½ bowl white rice. Stay away from breaded, fried meats, sweet and sour sauces, egg or spring rolls, spare ribs, fried rice.

Japanese: Eat everything except tempura; ½ bowl rice.

Mexican: Eat diet-sized portions of meat, chicken, or fish; side orders of beans, rice, salad, burritos, tamales, enchiladas; gazpacho and clear soups. Avoid tacos and tostadas (they're fried), guacamole, sour cream and cheese garnishes, taco chips, and chimichangas.

Italian: Eat half portions of plain pasta dressed only with tomato sauce; plain meat, chicken, fish, shellfish, and soups, the vegetables in an antipasto. Avoid layered and filled pastas, cheese and cream sauces, breaded meat and vegetables, vegetables sautéed in oil and butter.

Middle Eastern: Eat stuffed grape leaves, broiled lamb or chicken, tabouli (bulgur and parsley salad), humus, eggplant, salads with feta cheese. Avoid felafel, moussaka, egg-drop soup, and honey-drenched desserts.

Continental and Conventional: Eat diet-sized portions of any meat, poultry, fish, lamb, or pork prepared without coating, stuffing, or heavy sauces; potato or rice without butter, cheese, or sour cream; salad with oil and vinegar dressing; plain vegetables, fruit, small roll. Or eat only the appetizer or soup, a salad, and then proceed directly to dessert. Ask for your appetizer to be served when the main course is served to others.

Salad Bars: For your first helping, take carrots, green pepper, tomatoes, cabbage, spinach, 1 tablespoon cottage cheese, 1 tablespoon chick peas, and fill up the spaces with cucumbers, lettuce, and radishes. Use low-calorie dressing. Eat one slice of bread, no butter. If tofu (bean curd) is available, substitute for cottage cheese and chick peas, if desired. For the second helping, fill your bowl with lettuce, alfalfa sprouts, cucumbers, radishes, celery, and use low-calorie dressing. Do not eat anything with mayonnaise or marinade or put on croutons, bacon bits, or wheat germ.

Entertaining

Don't entertain at home if you can avoid it. Every elaborate dinner party or brunch you give makes you vulnerable to the temptations of pre- and post-party nibbling. If you want to entertain at home, recognize the times you are most likely to overeat and take precautions. Cook simple foods that don't keep you in the kitchen for hours. Make low-calorie dishes. (It won't hurt your guests to be served a nonfattening meal.) Don't prepare too much food; you want to avoid leftovers. Don't cook your favorite dishes because you will end up eating most of them yourself.

Leftovers are like time bombs in your kitchen, except it is your will power that explodes. Do the following. Before the guests leave, go into the kitchen and wrap up any leftovers that will travel. Then, before people leave, hand them small packages of food. Most people will accept it, especially if the amount is small. Anything that can't be sent away should be frozen immediately or put into the garbage. It is very easy to forget about eating something that you have thrown away; it is almost impossible to forget about eating something that sits in your refrigerator and says, "Eat me."

Children and Their Foods

"How can I get rid of all the junk food the kids are always eating? They expect it to be there and complain that they aren't on a diet so why shouldn't they eat it? But if I know it is in the kitchen, I end up eating it. I just can't keep my hands off their chips and cookies."

Children's foods can be a problem. Although it is possible to wean your children away from these sugar-filled confections (see my book *Eating Your Way Through Life*, Raven Press, New York, 1979), doing so is stressful and perhaps should be avoided until after your diet is over. But you can prevent yourself from eating these foods by making the children responsible for purchasing and storing them. This is what you do: Tell your children that you need their help to stick to your diet. Even a very young child can understand and will be delighted to help you be "good." Take the children to the market so they can buy their own snack foods; give them money and meet them either at the check-out counter or, if they are old enough to handle the purchases, back at the car. Don't let them tell you what they bought. When you get home, stay in the car until they put away their groceries. Tell them that if you find them, the penalty will be that they can't eat them. You won't be able to find them.

Now, if you find yourself in the store ostensibly buying snacks for the kids, ask yourself what you are doing. You know the answer. You are buying them for yourself. Put them back.

Relatives

Relatives can be hazardous to a diet. "My mother never lets me alone. When we go to visit, she is feeding us from the minute we step into the house until we leave. She is convinced I will succumb to malnutrition unless I eat two helpings of everything."

You must have a relative like that. You don't want to offend or disappoint someone who takes great joy in feeding you. But you do want to lose weight. What should you do? Three things. Taste, talk, and take.

Taste everything you are offered, but only taste.

Praise the food wildly, extol the virtues of home cooking, but do not finish it. Instead of eating, talk. Talk as much as you can so that everyone else is finished eating and you still have something left on your plate. And then help clear the plates so you can surreptitiously remove the food.

Take home anything you are offered. Sending food packages home with one's children or other relatives gives people almost as much pleasure as feeding them in their own homes. It is as though a little part of the relative's home is going home with you. Divide the food into portion sizes compatible with your diet or, if it is too fattening to fit into the diet program, give it away. Regardless of what you do, call up the relative who gave you the food and thank her.

People

If your weight is obviously changing, others will discuss it. People comment on weight almost as much as they talk about the weather, and the content of their remarks can range as widely. Some will be delighted with your loss of weight, and others will regard it as a disaster.

One of my patients told me, "My friends hated my weight loss. When my husband died, I was about thirty pounds overweight and looked awful. A year later, I lost the weight and looked pretty good. I guess my friends thought their husbands would think that too, and they deliberately tried to get me to gain back the weight. One would say that I looked older now that I was thin, another would put the chocolates on the bridge table in front of me, and another would make me taste a new dessert she was cooking every time I went to visit."

The pleasure or pain others feel about your weight makes dieting very difficult at times, and it is tempting to fall back into the old patterns of eating to minimize conflicts with others about your weight. If a relationship was more comfortable when you were heavier, it can be very hard to deprive yourself of both food and the emotional support of a friend or spouse. This problem involves more than just not overeating; to resolve it may take the help of a professional weight counselor, or a self-help group of dieters, or the support of someone who believes in your efforts to lose weight.

Travel and Business Meals

Traveling and eating at business lunches, dinners, and receptions can make dieting very difficult. If there is a long sequence of eating away from home, consider going off the Carbohydrate Craver's Diet and simply trying to maintain the weight you have already lost. However, there are some tricks that will help you stay on the diet somewhat.

If you fly often, avoid eating the high-calorie airline food by brown bagging it. Take along lunches from the menu plan, or containers of yogurt, fruit, raisins, or hard cheese, crackers, carrots, and green peppers. Accept the diet soft drinks and tomato juice passed out by the flight attendants. If you are between destinations and have used up your cache of food from home, order, from the restaurant where you are breakfasting, some food for lunch, such as a bagel or muffin, a banana or orange or a container of yogurt. If you pass a take-out grocery store or delicatessen, go in and order a take-out sandwich or salad. As you sit on the plane munching your barbecued chicken wings, and eating your garden salad while chewing on a dill pickle, you may find several passengers salivating in your direction.

Always put some nonperishable food in your suitcase or briefcase in the event that you arrive at your destination after all restaurants are closed. Plain granola bars, small boxes of cereal, raisins, and cheese wedges and crackers travel well and also come in handy as a before-cocktail-party snack (so you won't overeat potato chips and sour-cream dip).

Dining at business meetings or conventions can cause your waistline to expand faster than your profits. Follow the menu plan for eating at conventional restaurants. Do not eat automatically because you are so intent on conducting your business that you don't notice what is on the plate in front of you. Before you start to eat, take a minute and push to the side of your plate all foods you have no intention of eating. Then don't touch them. Don't let the waitress put dessert in front of you — simply wave it away. If you are served unidentifiable or inedible food (because of its calorie content), eat whatever you can salvage and make plans to go to a restaurant as soon as the meal is over.

A friend described a scientific conference she had attended. "The last meeting I went to concluded with a banquet. We were served chicken Kiev, which turned out to be a chicken breast heavily coated with bread crumbs and fried. It was stuffed with butter. With it were string beans in cheese sauce, potato puffs, and salad drenched in Russian dressing. There was ice cream in a meringue shell for dessert. I unwrapped the chicken and ate whatever I could detach from the filling and coating, and picked on a roll. Then as soon as the dinner was over, my friends and I headed for a Japanese restaurant."

Vacations

Vacations and diets are usually incompatible. Vacations are times of self-indulgence, and diets are times of self-denial. Unless you are absolutely committed to losing weight without interruption, consider going off the diet during a vacation and giving in to small temptations. There are ways of indulging your eating desires and not gaining weight.

Skip meals. If you know in advance that a particular meal will be highly caloric, skip another meal that day. Or if you prefer an afternoon cup of coffee with whipped cream and a gooey pastry rather than a conventional lunch, don't eat lunch.

Eat wickedly expensive but very-low-calorie foods: lobsters, caviar, oysters, fat white European asparagus, freshly caught and grilled trout, smoked salmon.

A patient who goes on an annual Scandinavian vacation told me she always loses weight. "All I eat is smoked salmon, for breakfast, lunch, and dinner. I don't even eat desserts because I have a passion for the salmon and could never afford it at home."

Increase your activity level. Take advantage of museums, shopping, markets, and other sightseeing attractions to walk constantly. If your motel has a pool, swim before dinner. Go beachcombing rather than continually sunbathing. Rent a bike. The more calories you use up in activity, the less guilty you have to feel about dessert.

Be cautious about alcohol consumption, especially if your drinks are the sweet fruity type that come with an umbrella stuck in the glass. There are a lot of calories under that umbrella.

Most of these suggestions are, unfortunately, difficult to follow on one particular type of vacation — a cruise.

As a friend described it, "All you do is eat and eat and eat, all day and all night. Since you've paid for everything in advance, price doesn't slow you down and, indeed, you try to eat your money's worth. And you can't even exercise off the meals. How many times can you walk around the deck?"

In spite of my friend's tale of woe, you might consider just tasting a bit of everything, so you don't feel deprived. And most cruise ships have at least one swimming pool and an exercise room in which to work off calories. If these alternatives don't appeal to you, stay on land for your vacation, and you should do all right.

You may, of course, bring home more of you than you started with. Don't despair. As soon as you have a chance to restock the refrigerator, go on the Morning-After Diet. By the time your clothes are back from the dry cleaner's, the extra weight will be off.

13

When the Weight Loss Stalls

BETWEEN FOUR and six weeks after you start the Carbohydrate Craver's Diet, you may find that the rate of weight loss seems to have slowed down, or even stopped — in spite of the fact that you have been following the diet plan faithfully. The timing couldn't be worse. Just when you are getting bored with being on a diet and having fantasies about fried clams and cheesecake, it seems as if all your restraint isn't worth the effort.

Let's look at what is going on.

First of all, some of the weight you lost during the first few weeks of the diet was probably water weight. Even though this diet allows you to eat substantial amounts of carbohydrate, it is probably less than what you were eating before you began the diet. Now your body is undoubtedly retaining some water and, until you get rid of it, your scale will not register a loss of fat. Does this sound strange? It really isn't.

Fat doesn't just melt away; otherwise we could put ourselves into a microwave oven and be thin. When the fat in your fat cells is used for energy, it is converted to water and carbon dioxide. You breathe out the carbon dioxide, and you excrete the water through urination. Since it is the retained water that is being weighed, you won't be able to tell by the scale whether you have lost weight until you lose the water. (One trick is to try on something that was snug at the waist before you started dieting. Since you rarely retain much water around your waistline, if you are losing weight, the fit should be looser.)

Here are a few steps you can take to hasten the loss of water. Cut down on salty foods and on the amount of salt and salty condiments you use on your foods. Drink coffee or tea; the caffeine acts as a diuretic on some people, making them urinate more frequently. Finally, check your calendar. This won't hasten water loss but will tell you if some of that water retention is related to an anticipated period. Also check the fit of your rings and wrist watch. If they feel tight, it is a sure sign that your lack of weight loss is due to water retention. Finally, be patient. You are not a camel and you can't hold on to the water forever.

The other thing that is happening is that your body is becoming wise to your caloric manipulations. It regards your diet as a state of semistarvation and responds by becoming very conservative in how it uses the calories you are feeding it. There is a well-documented decrease in the body's use of energy for its basic metabolic functions after six to eight weeks of dieting. But eventually — and this may take a few weeks — the body adjusts to the new lower level of caloric intake and is not so thrifty in using those calories. And, of course, the more calories the body wastes, the more it must use up in the form of your stored fat.

There is one way to accelerate weight loss during this calorie-conservation period, and you know what it is. Yes, exercise. Exercise uses up calories; if your body is slowing down metabolically, you can speed up muscularly. However, it is your choice. People can lose weight simply sitting in a chair and watching their plants grow. But if you are like most people, you may not be willing to wait that long.

You can increase calorie use by formal exercise such as sports, or a programmed regime of running or walking or biking. Or you can increase the amount of moving you do during the day. Or do both.

If you are going to exercise, please check out the nature of the endeavor with your physician. If you have been sedentary, you should make sure that whatever you do is compatible with your heart and lung capacity and with the state of your back and knees. Starting a program under the supervision of a certified exercise instructor, as in the programs offered at YMCAs, prevents you from pacing yourself too fast at the beginning and allows you to build up endurance.

Do whatever is compatible with your athletic skill, time, money, and local climate. Try to pick an activity that you can do all year round so that changes in the weather do not produce convenient excuses for climbing back into that armchair.

"I love to bike but in the winter it's always just too snowy or icy or windy or cold," a patient told me.

"Have you considered an exercycle?" I asked.

"Oh, I have one. It's on our sun porch," she said.

"Well, is it too cold out there to use it?"

"Oh, no, it is a heated porch. Oh, I guess I could bike in the winter, couldn't I? Well, there goes another excuse."

The more frequently you move those muscles, the more rapidly the weight will come off. Vary your activities so that more time-consuming ones can be replaced by shorter versions when your time is limited. It is difficult to plan a leisurely game of tennis or golf when family and work responsibilities beckon. However, five minutes of jumping rope or a brisk twenty-minute walk to a mailbox can be just as useful in burning off the calories.

Exercise with others if you can't motivate yourself into doing it alone. Exercise classes, bowling, dancing, swimming (if you do it at the same time every day, you begin to recognize the faces in the pool), walking, or jogging with a friend or family member can be pleasurable for the social interaction they provide as well as for the pounds they take away.

What if you hate formal exercise? If the last time you were in a gym was in high school and then under duress? If no one is going to get you to put on a pair of sweat pants to jog around a track? The answer is to incorporate more physical activity into your everyday life. It's easy.

At home. Be inefficient in the house. Rearrange the kitchen so you have to walk continually to get the utensils and ingredients for meal preparation.

Don't pile stuff at the foot of stairs to save trips. Every time something has to go up, take it up.

Stop wheeling the trash to the street. Carry the barrels one at a time.

At work. Rearrange your office, if you work in one, so you have to walk to the wastepaper basket and to the phone and to the file cabinet, if this is possible.

Pace up and down when you are on the phone.

Use the rest room farthest from your office.

Climb stairs whenever possible.

Park your car as high up in the garage as you can and walk down.

Get off one subway stop from your usual one so you have to walk farther to work.

Use lunchtime to do errands. Walk to the bank or to the store.

At any time. If you need a quart of milk or a newspaper, walk or bike to stores within a mile and a half of your home rather than drive.

Pick up litter. It is good for the waistline.

Sweep the sidewalk, garage, cellar, steps.

Garden, rake leaves, mow the lawn, shovel snow, wash the car.

Go to museums and walk around rather than to the movies to sit. Window-shop, roam around flea markets, zoos, public gardens, shopping malls.

Solicit funds for a favorite charity by walking to your neighbors' homes.

Volunteer at a hospital or old-age home and deliver flowers to the rooms or take people around.

Become a tour guide at a museum or historical house.

Every movement will help move that fat out of the fat cells. And, despite your grumblings about the boredom, pain, tedium, and unpleasantness of exercise, you may find that you actually feel better when you are doing some. Many people find that any kind of physical activity helps them to cope a little better, makes them feel a little more awake, or just puts them in a pleasanter mood.

I have a neighbor who runs. She told me that her husband can always tell whether she has run or not. "He told me that when I run, I walk around the house afterward singing to myself. When I don't run, I walk around the house complaining."

A Check List for Cheating

Sometimes a diet stalls or stops because a few hundred extra calories have somehow found their way into your stomach, every day. Not many. Just enough to offset the calorie deficit necessary for weight loss. If you are not retaining water, if you have begun to exercise, and you are still not losing weight, you should consider the possibility that you may be eating too much.

Please start weighing your food again. Just for a week. Be very careful about the amount of low-calorie foods you are eating. Even celery can produce a weight gain if you eat enough of it. Once you feel familiar with what the correct portion sizes should look like, you can stop the weighing and measuring.

How much nibbling are you doing? Are you

starting to buy foods for other members of the family that you like to eat? And are you perhaps eating them? Are you starting to bake again, or prepare elaborate dinners so you can do some tasting? And what is happening to those leftovers? Are they being left in your stomach?

One way to tell how much additional food you are eating is to write down everything you eat. The problem with that method is that either you stop eating the foods for that day or two or you get angry and eat even more. One of my patients had failed to lose weight for weeks. She kept showing me these perfect food records (her idea, not mine) for Mondays through Fridays. But never on weekends. She would always "misplace" those records. Finally, she admitted that she ate continually on weekends and felt too guilty and angry to write down what she was eating.

A compromise is to scribble down at the end of the day everything you remember putting into your mouth. The list will not be accurate, but it will give you some idea of how much nibbling is going on without being too stressful. If you have a tape recorder, use that for record keeping for a few days. Play it back and then erase the tape. Knowing what kinds of foods are tempting you to nibble will help you avoid them.

Become sensitive to what you are eating at work or socially. Some work situations are extremely difficult for a dieter because either co-workers or clients bring food and insist that everyone taste some. Or else someone is always leaving or having a baby or getting married, and lunchtime is a never-ending series of parties. If someone offers you food, refuse it graciously — but refuse it. And if you find that those lunches are depleting only your wallet and not your weight, then try to go to fewer of them, or suggest places like salad bars or seafood restaurants where you can eat a low-calorie meal.

Finally, don't despair. If you adhere to the diet, increase your physical activity, and decrease your cheating, the pounds will start to vanish again. Soon you will be as thin as you want to be. And you will have reached the end of the diet without ever feeling hungry for carbohydrates.

14

Preventing the Postdiet Inflation

"I always had this fantasy about weighing 120 pounds. I got down to that
weight, for about three hours. But then
my weight shot up to 128 immediately
and there it remains. Unless I fast or
get a stomach virus, I can't budge it."
— *A patient*

THE TIME to go off the Carbohydrate Craver's Diet
is when you feel physically and psychologically
comfortable in doing so. You should end the diet
even before reaching a specific target weight if you
are happy with your shape and size and look and
feel distinctly different from your prediet self. Target weights are often unrealistically low, and even
though the weight may drop to that level, it will
climb again by 5 or 10 pounds to a more comfortable level. Your maintenance weight may not be
reached until you are off your diet for several

weeks. It sometimes takes that long for your body to adjust to your slightly increased postdiet food intake and also to whatever exercise level you are sustaining. Do not be alarmed if the scale goes up and down somewhat like an airplane coming in for an aborted landing. As long as you remain in control of your eating and do not take on the activity level of a footstool, your weight will settle down.

It is better to use clothes, rather than the scale, as the measure of weight changes. When the diet is over, select a set of clothes that fit well. Try them on at least once a week to monitor changes in shape and size. If you notice that it is slightly harder to button a blouse or that the belt buckle is not as far over as it was, then get on the scale to see what has happened. You also should throw away all your expandable clothes: wraparound skirts, smocks, tent dresses, caftans, loose bathrobes, baggy corduroy pants, loose-fitting sweat pants. Otherwise, when you feel yourself inflating, you will start to wear them again in an attempt to conceal the problem from yourself as well as others.

The diet should end when you feel mentally comfortable about your shape and size. Because the Carbohydrate Craver's Diet produces a slow, steady weight loss, your shape should change at a rate that allows you to accept your new appearance. However, it is possible for you to reduce to a shape that is totally incompatible with the way you think of yourself: You may think of yourself as a sedan and find yourself looking like a sports car. If this happens, do not be surprised if you gain some weight despite your resolve not to. It is easier to hold on to and take care of something familiar than something alien.

Many people who have a great number of pounds to lose are more successful when they lose weight in stages, separated sometimes by months or even years. They become familiar with a new, thinner shape, live with it for a while, and then can accept the idea of being yet even thinner. Consider doing this if you stop the diet 20 or 30 pounds above the best weight for you because at the moment you are uncomfortable about looking any thinner.

Often the diet is ended not because a weight goal has been reached but rather because, like Mac-Arthur's old generals, it starts to fade away. Self-control and discipline begin to fray, and resistance and anger toward continuing the diet increase. If this begins to occur, stop the diet immediately. Redirect whatever self-discipline and motivation you have left toward maintaining your weight loss. You must make the decision to stop dieting consciously. Do not let the sight of increasing poundage on the scale make it for you.

Ending a diet means an end to the restrictions and limitations that influenced your food choices when you were losing weight. However, you still must control your eating and doing so means obeying some rules. Reaching your weight goal is a little like getting a driver's license: You no longer have to follow the suggestions and instructions of the teacher sitting beside you, but there are rules to be obeyed and you will find yourself in difficult situations for which you had no preparation. You assume that you may make some mistakes as a novice driver; assume also that you will make some mistakes as a novice thin person.

Everyone has had the experience of being told what to do when the car begins to skid and then having the car begin to skid and doing just the opposite. "Of course, I put on the brakes and tried to steer away from the skid, and of course the car skidded more."

You also have read the suggestions for maintaining your weight loss and handling the obstacles that might prevent your success. Accept the possibility that acting on them may be harder than reading about them, and have confidence that maintaining weight loss becomes easier with time and experience. Fortunately, it is easier and less costly to fix a bulging stomach then a dented fender.

The following guidelines will help, but experience will help even more.

1. Continue to follow the Carbohydrate Craver's Diet plan and add 500 calories to your daily intake. Do so by adding all the calories to one meal, or by adding extra calories to each meal, or by eating a week's worth of extra calories over the weekend.

Eating 3500 *extra* calories in two days may seem difficult, but it can be accomplished with ease, given the appropriate food choices. For example, a meal at a hamburger fast-food establishment can add up to:

Big Mac	571
French fries	211
Chocolate shake	324
Apple pie	295

Total: 1401 calories

If you decide to add calories to each meal, here is a simple way to do it:

Breakfast: Double the serving of cereal *or* bread *or* add a fruit

Lunch: Choose *two* of the following foods to add to lunch:

1 additional ounce of protein

1 ounce of cheese

1 cup of soup (noncream) and 2 small packages of saltines

1 serving of fruit

1 tablespoon nondiet salad dressing *or* 1 tablespoon butter or margarine *or* 1 tablespoon regular mayonnaise *or* 1 tablespoon
peanut butter, sour cream, or cream cheese

1 large bagel *or* roll instead of Syrian bread
pocket

1 cup plain low-fat yogurt *or* 1 percent fat
cottage cheese

Dinner: Choose *two* of the following foods to
add to dinner:

1 additional ounce of protein

1 tablespoon butter, sour cream, salad oil,
mayonnaise, regular salad dressing, margarine, peanut butter, *or* cream cheese
double serving size of rice *or* pasta *or* other
grain food

1 large *or* 2 small potatoes

8 ounces beer *or* 1½ ounces gin *or* 6 ounces
white wine *or* 100 calories' equivalent of
other alcoholic beverages

½ ounce cheese and 3 Triscuits

1 roll

1 fruit

2. Make sure that you weigh or measure the
foods you are adding to the meal and that you know
their caloric content. Buy a comprehensive and cur-

rent calorie book and check the number of calories in the amount of food you are planning to eat. Do not assume that ice cream with a high butter-fat content has the same number of calories as supermarket ice cream, or that whipped cream contains only air. Be especially cautious of concealed calories in sauces, batters, pie crusts, and fried foods.

Recently, I had dinner with a friend who had just successfully completed a diet. "I think I'll order some fried clams — they look good," he said, pointing to a plate being carried by.

"Are you sure?" I asked, remembering his struggles to lose weight.

"Why not? Clams don't have many calories."

"You're right, they don't, but the batter they're dipped in and the fat they're fried in do."

"Oh, well, maybe I'll have them steamed instead."

You will almost invariably eat too many calories soon after you complete the Carbohydrate Craver's Diet. Don't panic and don't feel guilty. Do what the rest of the thin world does: Eat less the next day. Go back to one of the diet plans or consciously restrict the amount of food you choose. The caloric overload is not irreversible.

3. Continue to eat the carbohydrate snack each day during your peak carbohydrate-craving period. It is not necessary to eat the same snack each day; however, follow the same cautions suggested earlier, such as avoiding addicting foods or foods high in fat or homemade foods whose size may vary from batch to batch. Be sure you eat at least 25 grams of carbohydrate and do not consume more than 200 calories.

4. If your weight starts increasing, scrutinize your eating habits carefully. Weigh all your food, not just new items you add to your daily food selection. Write down everything you are eating and nibbling — everything, especially on the bad days when you seem to be eating all the time. Be honest, because you are the only benefactor — no one will give you a prize for a good record or a scolding for a bad. Add up the calories each day and note, by circling the foods, where the extra calories are coming from. If you do not do this, you will have no idea how you are increasing your calorie intake and how you can modify your eating habits to prevent the weight gain.

5. Don't skip meals or become casual about their nutrient content. Continue to eat the Super Salads or other salads with similar ingredients and con-

tinue to drink milk or eat other dairy products. Keeping your body well nourished is as important as keeping it thin.

6. Continue to exercise. If you have managed to avoid any exercise during the diet, now is the time to start some form of routine physical activity. Your shape really will improve, and with your new weight loss, you will be able to wear some classy exercise clothes. If you give up the exercise you did during the diet, you may find yourself gaining weight.

7. Put away thoughts of reverting back to your prediet eating habits. That behavior is over, forever. The uncontrolled, uninhibited, "promiscuous" way of eating that may have caused you to gain weight in the past is behind you now. You should consider a return to that way of eating as unacceptable as eating baby food. You are a different person now, and your new style of eating must be compatible with the new shape you have developed. The old you would have looked at the rows of pastries displayed in a bakery shop or smelled the pizza baking in a neighborhood pizza parlor and said, "Why not, I'm fat anyway. What difference do a few extra (hundred) calories make?" The new you looks, and smells longingly, at these culinary enticements, and then walks on, knowing that those few extra (hundred) calories make a very big differ-

ence. You are in the driver's seat now, and you must exercise control, caution, and restraint.

One of my patients said, "Sometimes I find myself becoming sad when I think of all those foods I used to enjoy that I can no longer eat. Really, I have food fantasies about eating three or four pepperoni sandwiches, followed by an Italian cream-cheese pie and then those special cookies we eat at Christmas. But I realize I can't have it both ways. I don't want to weigh 270 pounds anymore, and that is more important to me than eating the foods that made me that way."

---

8. Find new pleasures to replace the pleasure eating used to give you. Seek out social and recreational activities that were incompatible with an earlier, fatter life. Develop a set of friends who know you only as a thin person. They will help you believe that you are thin because it will be difficult for them to think of you otherwise. If you associate only with those who knew you as heavier, your self-image will remain that of a fat person.

I have a friend who lost weight when he went away to college about twenty-five years ago. Some of his relatives whom he sees infrequently still remember him as a quite overweight adolescent. The first remark out of their mouths when he encounters them is "Oh, look at all the weight you've lost." He restrains himself from telling them how much they have gained.

———

9. Avoid using the threat of weight gain as a means of winning battles. Deliberately overeating in front of someone who has angered or frustrated you or announcing that you will do so can be an effective way of producing agreement or capitulation to your argument. The other person doesn't want to undermine your success in becoming thin and will feel very guilty and anxious if he thinks he is doing just that. You are the one to suffer the most ultimately because you have deliberately relinquished control over your eating. And the more you do this, the harder it will be to resume control later. And eventually you will overeat, regardless of whether it is part of your battle plan or not.

———

A computer scientist explained, "Whenever I got really angry at my wife, I would go into the kitchen and deliberately start to eat. She would become frantic because she was really afraid I would gain back all the weight I had lost. I would get my way, but I realize now what a childish thing I was doing. We went to some family counseling and learned to talk, not eat, out our problems."

If you find old, emotionally influenced patterns of overeating recurring, consider seeking professional help. Do it before you regain the weight you have lost.

Fat-Weather Friends

Some people stop feeling friendly toward you when you have acquired a smaller size. Be prepared for this; otherwise you will be hurt and bewildered at their non-pleasure in your weight-loss success. Do not expect them to compliment you on your new figure or wardrobe; they will comment only if they think you have gained back a few pounds or if your clothes look a little tight. The reasons for this attitude are many and can range from simple jealousy to a belief that the relationship you had with them when you were fat is now being threatened. Handle these unwelcome responses by seeking out others who are truly delighted with your new appearance, by diminishing attention to your weight loss when you are with the "fat-weather friends," and by asking a close friend or relative who is clearly disturbed by your weight loss to consider talking over his problem with someone who can give good advice.

15

Diet Questions and Answers

I HOPE you'll have found most of the answers to your questions in the previous chapters of this book. But here are some of the ones my patients and others who have learned about our work at MIT most often ask me:

Q. I thought sugar was bad for you. Should I try to choose a starchy instead of a sweet snack, even though I like sweets?

A. Sugar is bad for you *only* if you eat sugary foods instead of nutritious ones. Since you will be receiving all the daily nutrients you need from your meals, you don't have to worry about this. However, sugary foods can increase the formation of cavities, so you should brush your teeth after you snack. Otherwise, sugar is harmless.

Q. Why don't you have ice cream on the snack list? That's my favorite food.

A. Unfortunately, ice cream contains so much fat that you will go over your 200-calorie limit before you obtain the carbohydrate your body needs. When you feel an insatiable drive to eat some ice cream, eat one small scoop instead of your regular snack, and eat it slowly. Never buy ice cream in large quantities. You will eat it all at once.

Q. Why can't I eat a different snack every day?
A. Eating the same snack for at least two weeks teaches you to distinguish between a desire to eat something because it tastes good and because it satisfies your carbohydrate craving. The monotony of eating the same snack removes the desire to eat it because of its taste alone. When you eat it and feel satisfied, it is because your carbohydrate hunger is satisfied, not just your taste buds.

Q. Some days I don't feel like eating any snack. Is that bad for the diet?
A. No. There will be days when your carbohydrate hunger is very small and satisfied by the carbohydrate you eat at meals. As long as you always eat a carbohydrate snack during your peak craving period when you do feel the carbohydrate hunger, it is all right to skip the snack when you don't feel the need to eat one.

Q. Why am I the only one in my family who wants to eat sweets? Is there something wrong with me?

A. No. People are different. Perhaps you need more sleep than someone else in your family, or someone else is always more thirsty. There is nothing right or wrong with your hunger for sweets; it is simply the way your body works.

Q. If eating carbohydrate is so important, why do so many diet plans eliminate it?

A. There are two reasons for this. By eliminating or severely restricting carbohydrate, a diet plan will cause you to lose a lot of water weight early on in the diet, which will make you believe the diet is successful in making you thin. Also, there is a notion that the only way to make a carbohydrate overeater lose weight is to take away all carbohydrates. As you know, this works about as well as taking away water from someone who is always thirsty.

Q. Is there such a thing as an appetite for protein or fat?

A. Scientists have discovered that animals have a definite appetite for protein-rich foods and that during pregnancy, animals increase their appetite for high-fat foods. However, this phenomenon has not really been studied in people, although one woman told me she could tell when she was pregnant because she always developed a craving for whipped cream.

Q. I know the diet is the best one for me because I am a carbohydrate craver, but I want to lose weight really fast. What if I go on one of those crash diets first, lose some weight, and then start on yours?
A. That is not a good idea. The crash diets work because they eliminate carbohydrates and provide about 800 calories a day. No attention is paid to the nutritional adequacy of the diet, and certainly no attention is paid to whether your carbohydrate hunger is satisfied. It won't be. You may lose the weight rapidly, but you will also lose your ability to control your carbohydrate consumption. So going on the Carbohydrate Craver's Diet will be very difficult, since the controls in your brain that monitor your carbohydrate eating won't work well, and you may find yourself overeating carbohydrates. You can lose all the weight you need to lose on the Carbohydrate Craver's Diet.

Q. I love starchy foods like muffins, toast, and hot biscuits, but I really love them drenched in butter. Can I eat them that way?
A. No. Unfortunately, butter, or any other fat-based spread like cream cheese or peanut butter,

adds so many calories that it is almost impossible to
stay within the caloric limit for snacks. When you
stop dieting, and can eat some more calories, then
you can put these spreads on your snacks. You must
always be aware of how much you are eating; however, don't exceed one or one and a half tablespoons. Otherwise, you will be back on the diet.

Q. Why are most of the cookies I like best not on
the snack list?

A. Two reasons. First, many cookies are made
with considerable amounts of shortening or lard,
which make them very high in calories (even
though they don't taste it). So it may be hard to get
the carbohydrate you need without exceeding your
200-calorie limit. Second, it is almost as hard to eat
only one cookie as to eat only one potato chip: Your
carbohydrate hunger is filled, your stomach is full,
but your mouth keeps saying "More, more." So the
cookies on the snack list are chosen because they
are not among the top ten of cookie favorites and
are easier to stop eating.

Appendixes

Publications by
Judith J. Wurtman

FOR THE GENERAL READER

Wurtman, Judith J.
1978. "Eating During Childhood and Adolescence."
Parents Magazine, March.
"Food Additives." *Harvard Medical School
Health Letter*, October.
1979. "The American Eater." *Vital Issues* 29, Center
for Information on America.
Eating Your Way Through Life. New York:
Raven Press.
1980. "Eating on the Run." *Wellesley Alumnae Magazine*, Winter.
"Vitamin and Mineral Supplementation." *Harvard Medical School Health Letter*, June.
1982. "New Views on Feeding Babies." *Harvard Medical School Health Letter*, August.

RELATED SCIENTIFIC PUBLICATIONS

Wurtman, J. J.; Moses, P.; and Wurtman, R. J.
1982. "Prior Carbohydrate Consumption Affects the
Amount of Carbohydrate Rats Choose to Eat."
Journal of Nutrition (accepted for publication).

Wurtman, J. J., and Wurtman, R. J.

1977. "The Effect of Fenfluramine and Fluoxetine on Food Intake of Rats." *FASEB Abstracts,* April.

1979. "Drugs That Enhance Central Serotoninergic Transmission Diminish Elective Carbohydrate Consumption by Rats." *Life Science* 24:895–.

"Fenfluramine and Other Serotoninergic Drugs Depress Food Intake and Carbohydrate Consumption While Sparing Protein Consumption." *Current Medical Research Opinion* 6, Suppl. 1:28–33.

"Sucrose Consumption Early in Life Fails to Modify the Appetite of Adult Rats for Sweet Foods." *Science* 205:321–322.

1981. "Neurotransmitter Regulation of Protein and Carbohydrate Consumption." In *Nutrition and Aging,* ed. H. Munro. Boston: New England University Press.

"Suppression of Carbohydrate Intake from Snacks and Meals by d-l-Fenfluramine and Tryptophan." In *Anorectic Drugs: Mechanisms of Action and Tolerance,* ed. S. Garattini. New York: Raven Press.

Carbohydrate Craving in Obese People: Suppression by Treatments Affecting Serotoninergic Transmission[1]

Judith J. Wurtman, Ph.D.,[2]
Richard J. Wurtman, M.D.,
John H. Growdon, M.D.,
Peter Henry, Anne Lipscomb, M.A., and
Steven H. Zeisel, M.D., Ph.D.[3, 4]

ABSTRACT

We examined the existence of carbohydrate cravings, and the effects on such cravings of treatments that enhance serotonin release, among twenty-four obese subjects who claimed to have excessive appetites for carbohydrates. Subjects living in a college dormitory for four weeks were given three fixed meals daily and allowed to choose at

Laboratory of Neuroendocrine Regulation, Department of Nutrition and Food Science, Massachusetts Institute of Technology, Cambridge, MA 02139

1. Tryptophan studies supported by grants from the National Institutes of Health (AM-14228); fenfluramine studies supported by the Center for Brain Sciences and Metabolism Charitable Trust.
2. Author to whom reprint requests should be addressed at MIT room 56-245, Cambridge, MA 02139.
3. Dr. Judith J. Wurtman, research associate, is a cell biologist and

will among five protein-rich or five carbohydrate-rich isocaloric snack foods, provided via a vending machine. For two weeks, they received no treatment (study 1) or a placebo (study 2); for the next two weeks, they received placebo, d-l-fenfluramine, or l-tryptophan.

All but one of the subjects exhibited a marked preference for carbohydrate-rich over protein-rich snacks during the first two weeks of the study. The average daily intake of carbohydrate-rich snacks was 4.1 ± 0.4 and of protein-rich snacks 0.8 ± 0.3. Seventeen of the subjects failed to consume any protein snacks on most days during the baseline or test periods, thus it was not possible for us to examine the effect of test treatments on protein snack intake. Fenfluramine administration significantly reduced carbohydrate snacking in six of nine test subjects, as well as in the group as a whole (2.4 ± 0.6 snacks/day vs. 4.2 ± 0.6 during the two-week baseline period). Tryptophan significantly diminished carbohydrate intake in three of the eight treated subjects, and increased it in one subject; it did not significantly modify snacking patterns in the group as a whole. Placebo administration did not affect carbohydrate intake in any of the seven test subjects.

---

nutritionist who does research on brain mechanisms regulating food intake.

Dr. Richard J. Wurtman is the director of the Laboratory of Neuroendocrine Regulation.

Drs. John Growdon and Steven Zeisel are, respectively, a neurologist and pediatrician interested in the effects of nutrients on brain function.

Peter Henry is a computer consultant.

Anne Lipscomb is a dietician.

4. Dr. Zeisel is a John A. and George L. Hartford Fellow of the John A. Hartford Foundation.

These observations show that some obese people do consume carbohydrate-rich snacks frequently and preferentially, and that this behavior can sometimes be diminished by treatments thought to enhance serotonin's release (fenfluramine) or synthesis (tryptophan).

INTRODUCTION

Consumption of a high-carbohydrate, low-protein diet for one to two hours accelerates serotonin synthesis in and release from the brain neurons of fasting rats (Fernstrom and Wurtman, 1971; Wurtman et al., 1981). The carbohydrate elicits insulin secretion, which markedly reduces plasma levels of most large, neutral amino acids (LNAA) but not of tryptophan (Wool, 1965; Fernstrom and Wurtman, 1972a; Fernstrom et al., 1979). The resulting change in the plasma tryptophan/LNAA ratio facilitates tryptophan's uptake into the brain (Fernstrom and Wurtman, 1971; Pardridge, 1977), thereby increasing the saturation of tryptophan hydroxylase, the enzyme that controls serotonin synthesis (Carlsson and Lindqvist, 1978). Protein intake blunts or may even reverse this effect, because dietary proteins contribute much larger quantities of the other LNAAs than of tryptophan to the plasma (Fernstrom et al., 1979); a high-protein meal thus actually reduces brain tryptophan and serotonin levels (Fernstrom and Wurtman, 1972b). The acceleration of brain serotonin synthesis after a carbohydrate-rich meal might affect mechanisms that control appetite, especially appetite for carbohydrates (Wurtman and Wurtman, 1977; Wurtman and Wurtman, 1979). That carbohydrate consumption is, indeed, controlled, and by a mechanism distinct from that regulating protein intake, has been shown for the rat (Wurtman and Wurtman, 1977). Moreover, the participation of brain serotonin in this mechanism has been demonstrated by studies showing that carbohydrate intake by animals allowed to choose among foods that differ in nutrient content is preferentially suppressed by drugs that enhance serotoninergic neurotransmission (Wurtman and Wurtman, 1977; Wurtman and Wurtman, 1979). Presumably, the increase in serotonin synthesis that follows carbohydrate intake acts similarly, diminishing the likelihood of continued carbohydrate intake. If so, it is conceivable that pathophysiologic changes in this complex metabolic-neurochemical-behavioral feedback mechanism might underlie some disorders of appetite regulation.

Certain obese people, and even people of average weight, describe powerful and frequent cravings for carbohydrate-rich foods. These cravings are reportedly exacerbated by stress (Lewis, 1980) or, in women, by premenstrual tension. In a study of 300 nurses, Smith and Saunders (1969) found an association between premenstrual tension and cravings for sweet foods. The consumption of carbohydrate-rich foods may fill a metabolic as well as a sensory need, i.e., by raising the plasma tryptophan/LNAA ratio, carbohydrate ingestion may accelerate brain serotonin synthesis (Wurtman et al., 1981). Conceivably, excessive carbohydrate cravings reflect inadequate serotoninergic neurotransmission, and a learned desire to consume foods that will enhance serotonin synthesis and release. If so, then pharmacological treatments designed to amplify serotonin release might, in some subjects, ameliorate this appetite disorder. We initially tested this hypothesis using a group of nonobese outpatients (Wurtman and Wurtman, 1981). Their claimed propensity for carbohydrate snacking was confirmed and, in some individuals, shown to be suppressed by treatment with d-l-fenfluramine, a drug thought to release serotonin into brain synapses (Fuller et al., 1978), or with l-tryptophan. The present study examines the possibility that these treatments might also diminish carbohydrate intake in some obese inpatients allowed *ad libitum* access to high-carbohydrate or high-protein snack foods provided via a computer-operated vending machine.

MATERIALS AND METHODS

Recruitment and Screening of Subjects

Advertisements including the phrases "carbohydrate craver" and "overweight" were used to attract obese individuals to the study. Respondents were sent a questionnaire about their weight history, general health, and snacking patterns. Those who reported a tendency to snack on high-carbohydrate foods when not hungry, and who were in good health, not currently on any medication, and overweight according to standard height-weight charts (New York Metropolitan Life Insurance Co., 1959) were invited to an orientation session. They were given a physical examination and a detailed interview about their eating habits. Subjects who did not specifically overeat high-carbohydrate foods were excluded at this time. Permission was obtained for participation in the study from subjects who passed the physical examination. All subjects who were accepted into the study claimed to snack frequently on high-carbohydrate foods.

Two four-week studies were done (July and August

1980). Fifteen females and two males were accepted into the first study (Table I). One subject left the study early because of a death in the family, and another (X) was asked to leave due to failure to comply with the protocol; their data were not used. A third subject (Ji.La.) left at the beginning of the fourth week because of a legal problem; data from his first three weeks were used.

One male and eleven females were accepted into the second study (Table I). One (E.N.) left early due to sickness; her data were not used. Two others (XX and XXX) participated in the study, but their data were not used because of noncompliance with the protocol. Subjects lived in an MIT dormitory and ate all of their food in a study-designated dining area. Subjects were not allowed to work during the four weeks except for G.N., who was completing a part-time teaching position.

Meals

Meals were designed to meet daily nutrient needs. In the first study, the daily caloric content was 1200 calories during the first three weeks and 950 during the final week; for the second study meals provided 950 calories throughout. (Based on the extremely limited physical activity of the subjects during the four-week study, and on food intake records provided before the study, we estimated that they needed to consume between 1600 and 2000 calories daily to maintain their weight. Thus they could consume from 700 to 1400 calories of snack foods and still maintain their weight.) The nutrient composition of the meals corresponded to that of a typical American diet. In the first study, the total calories from

TABLE I: Subject Profile

Name	Height	Starting weight (lb)	End weight (lb)	Age (yr)	Sex
Study 1					
F.B.	5'4"	144	142	59	f
D.C.	5'3"	192	190	54	f
B.D.	5'6"	162	161	31	f
M.B.	5'6"	190	191	42	f
K.N.	5'6"	217	215	64	f
J.R.	5'7"	265	264	32	f
P.A.	5'6"	176	174	19	f
A.L.	5'10"	252	240	48	m
Ja.La.[1]	6'2"	258	264	47	m
G.H.	5'2"	150	153	66	f
D.B.	5'5"	218	220	60	f
D.K.	6'2"	302	312	20	f
K.L.	5'8"	150	153	23	f
C.S.	5'1"	163	164	50	f
E.N.	5'5"	175	174	52	f
X[3]	5'4"	177	178	30	f
B.T.[2]	5'9"	260	264	31	f
Study 2					
M.K.	5'5"	170	168	56	f
J.L.	5'2"	141	140	27	f
B.C.	5'3"	167	164	42	f
L.H.	5'1"	161	163	52	f
Mi.Ri.	5'4"	182	182	50	f
D.D.	5'6"	216	214	43	f
D.T.	5'6"	214	216	50	f
XX[3]	5'2"	187	188	58	f
Ma.Ri.	5'6"	220	219	49	m
XXX[3]	5'5"	234	237	39	f
G.N.	5'2"	182	180	30	f
E.N.	5'2"	139	139	65	f

1. Left study during third week.
2. Left study during second week; data not included.
3. Subjects dropped from study for failure to comply with protocol.

protein, carbohydrate, and fat equaled 19, 46, and 32%, respectively; in the second study, these were 23, 47, and 30%.

Subjects had no choice of foods at mealtime. One subject in each study reported that the meals contained too many calories to permit a constant level of snacking; hence, their mealtime calories were diminished on day 3 (to 950 for F.B., study 1, and to 750 for B.C., study 2).

Caffeine-containing beverages were allowed only at mealtimes; no carbonated beverages were permitted.

A refrigerated, rented vending machine (Seiler Corp., Waltham, MA) located in the dining area contained five high-protein and five high-carbohydrate snacks, each providing 165 to 179 calories (Table II). All prepared

TABLE II: Vending Machine Snack Foods			
Food	*Calories*	*Protein* (g)	*CHO* (g)
Ham and cheese	165	15	0
Potato chips	160	1	14
½ Bagel and cream cheese	160	4	21
Meatballs	179	16	4[3]
Chocolate chip cookies	175	1	20
Salami and cheese	160	9	0
M & M candies	175	0	21
Barbecued pork chops	160	16	4[4]
Chocolate cupcake[1]	160	2	25
½ Cranberry muffin[2] and butter	175	3	20
3 Cocktail frankfurters	165	7	1

Foods are listed in the same vertical order as their placement in the vending machine.
1. Used in Study 1.
2. Used in Study 2.
3. CHO is from catsup and breadcrumbs in meatball mixture.
4. CHO is from barbecue sauce.

foods were carefully weighed to ensure constancy of size and caloric content.

To familiarize the subjects with the snacks before the start of the experiment, a buffet dinner containing all of the snacks was served on the evening before the study began.

Access to the Vending Machine

The vending machine was operated by a microcomputer, Ohio Scientific, C4PMF (Ohio Scientific, Aurora, OH). To obtain food, each subject entered a personal three-digit access code into the computer; when the code was entered, all ten windows in the vending machine unlatched. When the subject opened one window and removed the snack, the snack was replaced automatically and the other windows locked. The computer recorded which snack was chosen and the time of its removal. At the end of the study, a computer printout was made indicating the time that each snack had been taken, its identity, and its carbohydrate, protein, and total caloric contents. (Subjects were given a copy of this printout.)

Subjects were allowed to remove as many snacks as they desired; however, they could not remove more than one during any five-minute period, share snacks, or obtain them for others. The snacks had to be eaten immediately after their removal from the vending machine. None could be taken from the machine at mealtimes or during the preceding thirty minutes. Although the subjects were told to keep their access code a secret, one subject in the second study (XXX) was discovered using the code of another subject (XX) to obtain food; hence, their food intake data could not be used.

We anticipated that subjects might eat food out of boredom if they were restricted to the dormitory and not allowed to participate in any activity. To prevent this, books, games, television, puzzles, and needlepoint kits were provided; an art teacher gave weekly lessons; and educational films and lectures were scheduled several times a week. Subjects were allowed to use campus athletic, recreational, library, and photographic facilities at will, and to attend campus movies, plays and concerts, and free public concerts in an adjacent park. Subjects could be away from the dormitory for ninety minutes at a time; at the end of each ninety-minute period, they were required to sign in with the computer. (This required typing in their code in response to a sign-in command on the computer screen.)

Experimental Procedures

Maintenance of weight. Subjects were told that they were not supposed to lose weight deliberately during the study, since any planned reduction in caloric intake or increase in physical activity would make it difficult to define the subject's normal snacking patterns or to evaluate the effects of test treatments on carbohydrate intake. Diet counseling was offered at the end of the study and at follow-up sessions one, three, and six months later. To ensure compliance with this restriction on weight loss, subjects were weighed weekly. Subjects exhibiting fluctuations in weight greater than 5 pounds were questioned about their eating and exercise patterns. One subject (X) was asked to leave the study when it was discovered that she had put fish weights in her pockets to obscure her deliberate attempt to lose weight.

Treatment. Drugs and placebos were taken immediately after meals (9:30 A.M., 1:00 P.M., and 6:00 P.M.). Lactose, used as the placebo, was administered in three equally divided doses totaling 2.3 grams daily. Tryptophan and fenfluramine were also administered in three equally divided doses. The total daily dose of tryptophan was 2.4 grams; that of fenfluramine was 60 milligrams in the first study and 45 milligrams in the second. (The fenfluramine dose was decreased to prevent the slight drowsiness reported by a few subjects in the first study.) D-l-fenfluramine was provided by the Servier Co. (Paris, France), l-tryptophan by the Ajinomoto Co. (Tokyo, Japan), and lactose by the New England Medical Center Pharmacy (Boston, MA). All were put into similarly sized white gelatin capsules to prevent subjects from identifying the substances they were receiving. All subjects took the same number of capsules.

Schedule of Drug Administration

The first four to five days of the study were used to accommodate the subjects to the new environment and eating situations, and the subsequent eight to nine days to provide baseline data on their snacking patterns. The treatment period began on day 14 and continued through day 28. In the first study, subjects received no treatment during the first two weeks. In the second, they were given placebo capsules in order to eliminate the novelty of taking capsules. (They were not informed that the capsules contained only placebo.) All subjects in both studies were told that they would be assigned randomly to one of the three treatment groups; subjects in the second study were told that some might be receiving both placebo and a drug during the course of the experiment while others would get only placebo. Subjects were assigned to each treatment group by one of the physicians responsible for their care. The assignments were made randomly and the study was carried out double-blind. Another physician who knew the treatment code was responsible for the general health of the subjects, but did not otherwise participate in study-related decisions. One subject, P.A., developed a skin rash after receiving fenfluramine for a week, and was switched to placebo for the second treatment week.

Data Analysis

The mean numbers of carbohydrate and protein snacks eaten daily by each subject were determined for the baseline and treatment periods, using data from days 5–13 and 15–26 for study 1 and days 4–13 and 15–25 for study 2. Data from studies 1 and 2 were pooled. The response of each experimental group to its treatment (placebo, fenfluramine, or tryptophan) was determined by calculating each subject's mean daily snack intakes during the baseline and treatment periods and then determining the group means for these periods; paired t-tests were used for this analysis. The magnitude of each subject's response to treatment was determined by comparing his or her daily snack intakes during the baseline and treatment periods; a nonpaired t-test was used for this analysis because the number of baseline and treatment days sometimes differed.

We anticipated that the dosages of fenfluramine or tryptophan would be short-acting (Woolsey et al., 1979; Kyriakides and Silverston, 1979; Blundell et al., 1979). Hence, for calculations of drug effects we used only the snacks consumed during the four to six hours after each of the three drug doses. By omitting from consideration the snacks consumed between midnight and breakfast, we dropped less than 5% of the total daily snack intake. A separate analysis of these data showed that snack intake during the period between midnight and breakfast did not differ among the three treatment groups.

Days 7–10 were not included in determining Ja.Li.'s baseline snack consumption since she had a viral illness during this period; day 18 was omitted from calculations of P.A.'s treatment responses since she was switched from fenfluramine to placebo on that day.

RESULTS
Weights

Three subjects showed weight changes of greater than 3 pounds during the four weeks of the study; A.L. lost 12 pounds, J.L. gained 6 pounds, and D.R. gained 10 pounds. Two subjects lost 3 pounds, two gained 3 pounds, thirteen lost between 1 and 2 pounds, five gained between 1 and 2 pounds, and one showed no change in weight.

Pattern of Carbohydrate and Protein Snack Consumption

The mean daily intake of carbohydrate snacks during the baseline period was 4.1 ± 0.4 and protein snacks 0.8 ± 0.3; these were not affected by placebo administration during this period. Thus the subjects consumed significantly more carbohydrate than protein snacks ($P < 0.001$). Two subjects, K.N. and C.S., ate no protein snacks at all during the baseline period and fifteen ate less than one per day. The very low consumption of high-protein snacks both affirmed the existence of a selective carbohydrate craving in our experimental subjects and precluded our examining possible effects of the test treatments on appetite for protein. The number of carbohydrate snacks consumed ranged from a low of one per day to a high of 10.5; most subjects consumed three to five per day. One subject, D.T., ate more protein snacks than carbohydrate snacks during the baseline period; she also consumed as many protein as carbohydrate snacks during the treatment period, when she received placebo.

We analyzed each subject's daily snack pattern to see if the snacks tended to be consumed during particular time periods or randomly throughout the day and evening. Five time periods were considered, i.e., before breakfast (5:00 A.M.–9:00 A.M.), between breakfast and lunch (9:30 A.M.–12:30 P.M.); lunch and dinner (1:00 P.M.–5:30 P.M.); evening (6:00 P.M.–10:00 P.M.), and late evening–early morning (10:00 P.M.–5:00 A.M.) The number of carbohydrate snacks consumed during each was determined for each baseline day and expressed as the mean percentage of total daily carbohydrate snack consumption (Table III). Too few subjects consistently ate protein snacks to allow a similar temporal analysis of protein snack consumption.

Four subjects tended to eat most of their carbohydrate snacks during the evening (M.B., E.N., C.S., and P.A.) and two (A.L. and Ja.Li.) consumed most during the late evening. Most subjects snacked repeatedly during both the afternoon and evening. No subject consumed a major portion of snacks during the morning.

TABLE III: Percentage of Daily Carbohydrate Snacks Consumed During Specific Daily Time Periods During Baseline Period

TIME OF DAY

Subjects	5:00 A.M.–9:00 A.M.	9:30 A.M.–12:30 P.M.	1:00 P.M.–5:30 P.M.	6:00 P.M.–10:00 P.M.	10:00 P.M.–5:00 A.M.
M.B.	0	11	37	51	0
E.N.	0	0	35	62	3
J.R.	0	14	40	42	4
B.C.	1.8	7	24	47	22
G.N.	4.5	12	27	21	35
F.B.	0	4	48	48	0
A.L.	0	7	27	20.6	45
D.T.	8	15	38	26	11.6
P.R.	2.5	15	33	43	18
D.C.	0	0	46	53	0
G.H.	0	8	31.5	39	21
D.K.	0	17	33	47	2.3
K.N.	0	13	36	46	3
Ma.Ri.	1.7	14	30	38	15.7
L.H.	0	4	36	26	24
Mi.Ri.	0	7.8	39	21	31
Ja.Li.	0	0	19	36	44
D.B.	0	0	54	45	0
K.L.	0	8.6	39.6	34	17
B.D.	0	0	38	46	15
C.S.	0	5	30	50	15
Ja.La.	0	15	24	36	24
P.A.	0	0	28	66	5
D.D.	0	15.6	37	39	8

Data show carbohydrate snack consumption as percentage of total snacks during the initial two-week period of the study. Placebo administration failed to modify the temporal pattern of snack intake during this period; hence data from the no-treatment and placebo periods were pooled.

Meals were served at 9:00 A.M., 12:30 P.M., and 6:00 P.M. No snacks were allowed during meals.

Effect of Placebo, Tryptophan, or
Fenfluramine on Snack Intake

Placebo. Placebo administration to seven subjects during the treatment phase of the study had no effect on carbohydrate intake (Table IV), either for the group as a whole or for any individual. Placebo treatment also failed to affect protein snacking (1.1 ± 0.58 snacks/day during the treatment period vs. 0.7 ± 0.37 protein snacks/day during the baseline period).

Fenfluramine. Fenfluramine treatment significantly reduced carbohydrate snack intake in the treatment group as a whole (P < 0.001) (Table V), and in six of the subjects (Mi.Ri., D.B., B.D., C.S., Ja.Li., and D.D.). Three of these

---

TABLE IV: Effect of Placebo on Carbohydrate Snack Consumption

| Subjects | CARBOHYDRATE SNACKS/DAY | |
	Control	Placebo
A.L.	3.0 ± 0.31	2.7 ± 0.39
F.B.	1.6 ± 0.33	1.4 ± 0.42
E.N.	3.2 ± 0.43	4.0 ± 0.28
J.R.	5.3 ± 0.27	7.4 ± 0.42
G.N.	3.0 ± 0.56	2.7 ± 0.47
D.T.	2.7 ± 0.57	2.7 ± 0.48
B.C.	2.3 ± 0.39	1.8 ± 0.18

Subjects A.L., F.B., E.N., and J.R. (study 1) received no treatment for the first two weeks and placebo (lactose 2.3 g/day in three divided doses) during the second two weeks. Subjects G.N., D.T., and B.C. (study 2) received placebo during both the first and second two-week periods. In all cases, subjects did not know whether pills given during either period would be placebo or treatment. Comparisons for each subject were made between mean snack intakes during days 4 or 5 through 13, and 15 through 25 or 26, respectively. Data are expressed as means ± S.E.M.

TABLE V: Effect of Fenfluramine on Carbohydrate Snack Consumption

| | CARBOHYDRATE SNACKS/DAY | |
Subjects	Control	Fenfluramine
K.L.	7.7 ± 0.42	5.7 ± 0.37 (n.s.)
D.B.	1.0 ± 0.02	0.1 ± 0.08 (P < 0.001)
P.A.	2.3 ± 0.33	1.8 ± 0.40 (n.s.)
B.D.	4.7 ± 0.53	1.1 ± 0.21 (P < 0.001)
Ja.La.	4.6 ± 0.90	2.3 ± 0.47 (n.s.)
C.S.	2.7 ± 0.27	0.8 ± 0.21 (P < 0.001)
Mi.Ri.	4.7 ± 0.42	3.1 ± 0.32 (P < 0.001)
Ja.Li.	5.1 ± 0.70	3.5 ± 0.43 (P < 0.05)
D.D.	5.1 ± 0.63	3.0 ± 0.66 (P < 0.05)

Subjects K.L., D.B., P.A., B.D., Ja.La., and C.S. (study 1) received no treatment for the first two-week period and fenfluramine (60 mg/day in three divided doses) during the second two weeks. P.A. received fenfluramine for six days and was then switched to placebo for seven days; during this period she ate 2.8 ± 0.54 carbohydrate snacks/day. Subjects Mi.Ri., Ja.Li., and D.D. (study 2) received placebo for the first two weeks and fenfluramine (45 mg/day in three divided doses) for the second two weeks. Comparisons for each subject (except for P.A.) were made between mean snack intake during days 4 or 5 through 13, and 15 through 25 or 26, respectively. Data are expressed as means ± S.E.M.

six people ate one or more protein snacks per day during the baseline period (Mi.Ri., D.D., and B.D.); two of them (Mi.Ri., D.D.) showed no significant changes in protein snacking while taking fenfluramine, while one (B.D.) decreased her protein snack intake significantly. The average number of protein snacks per day for the group was 1.17 ± 0.27 during pretreatment and 0.71 ± 0.26 when receiving fenfluramine.

Tryptophan. Three subjects showed a significant decrease in carbohydrate snack intake after tryptophan administration (Ma.Ri., L.H., and K.N.) (Table VI). Ma.Ri.'s carbohydrate snack intake ranged from three to seven snacks per day on placebo (study 2) and from one to four snacks per day on tryptophan. His protein intake also diminished slightly, from a baseline range of zero to three snacks per day to a treatment range of zero to two snacks per day; however, he consumed protein snacks consistently during both control and treatment periods. L.H. ate four to eleven carbohydrate snacks per day while on placebo, and four to six while on tryptophan; her range of protein snacks on placebo was zero to three snacks, and on tryptophan, zero to two. K.N. ate two to

TABLE VI: Effect of Tryptophan on Carbohydrate Snack Consumption

| Subjects | CARBOHYDRATE SNACKS/DAY | |
	Control	Tryptophan
D.K.	10.5 ± 1.10	13.0 ± 0.63 (n.s.)
G.H.	4.7 ± 0.63	7.5 ± 0.67 ($P < 0.01$)[1]
K.N.	4.0 ± 0.53	2.2 ± 0.35 ($P < 0.02$)
D.C.	2.4 ± 0.43	1.3 ± 0.22 (n.s.)
M.B.	3.1 ± 1.10	3.6 ± 1.00 (n.s.)
Ma.Ri.	4.4 ± 0.33	2.6 ± 0.29 ($P < 0.001$)
P.R.	4.0 ± 0.31	3.6 ± 0.28 (n.s.)
L.H.	6.6 ± 0.36	4.7 ± 0.34 ($P < 0.005$)

Subjects D.K., G.H., K.N., D.C., and M.B. (study 1) received no treatment for the first two weeks and tryptophan (2.4 g/day in three divided doses) during the second two weeks. Subjects Ma.Ri., P.R., and L.H. (study 2) received placebo during the first two-week period and tryptophan during the second two weeks (2.4 g/day in three divided doses). Comparisons for each subject were made between mean snack intakes during days 4 or 5 through 13, and 15 through 25 or 26, respectively. Data are expressed as means ± S.E.M.

1. Increased from control

seven carbohydrate snacks per day during the baseline
period, and one to five snacks per day on tryptophan; on
eleven of the thirteen test days, she ate only one or two
carbohydrate snacks per day. (K.N. did not eat any protein snacks during the baseline or treatment periods.)

One other subject, D.C., showed a consistent but not
significant reduction in carbohydrate snack consumption,
from one to four per day during the baseline period, to
zero to two while on tryptophan.

G.H. significantly increased her carbohydrate intake
during the tryptophan treatment period. This increase
primarily reflected a major increase in her consumption
of M & M candies during the final week of the study: she
consumed up to eight bags per day, commenting at the
end of the study that she wished to see how many bags
she needed to eat to satisfy her chocolate craving.

Although tryptophan did not produce a significant reduction in the consumption of carbohydrate snacks by
the group as a whole, it did have a significant effect in
three of the eight subjects (Table VI). Protein snack consumption for the group as a whole was 1.1 ± 0.27
snacks/day during the pretreatment period and 0.95 ±
0.28 during the treatment period.

Effect of Tryptophan or Fenfluramine on the Time of Carbohydrate Snack Consumption

No treatment significantly modified the temporal pattern
of snack consumption. Fenfluramine treatment delayed
the peak time of carbohydrate snacking in only one of the
responders, and this change (as reflected by the time of
day by which 50% of the carbohydrate snacks had been

eaten) involved only fifteen to thirty minutes. None of the subjects given placebo or tryptophan (including the three who decreased carbohydrate snacking after tryptophan) changed their times of peak carbohydrate snacking.

DISCUSSION

This study provides evidence that some overweight people who claim to crave carbohydrate-rich foods actually do manifest such cravings when given a choice between readily available, highly palatable carbohydrate- and protein-rich snacks. Moreover, the time of day when carbohydrate snacking is most likely to occur tends to be characteristic for each individual. Fenfluramine reduced significantly the number of carbohydrate snacks consumed in the treatment group as a whole and in six of nine subjects. Tryptophan significantly decreased carbohydrate snack consumption in three of eight subjects but not in the treatment group as a whole. Consumption of protein snacks could not be assessed in our experimental population of carbohydrate-craving obese people, since they consumed too few protein-rich snacks.

The low doses of fenfluramine used in this study (45–60 mg/day) are below those generally used to produce anorexia (Weinberger et al., 1978; Blundell et al., 1979; Kyriakides and Silverston, 1979) and did not cause significant weight loss among our subjects studied for fourteen treatment days. However, if the chronic use of such doses allows carbohydrate intake to continue to be reduced to the extent observed here (i.e., from 4.2 to 2.4 snacks/day, with a net reduction in daily caloric intake of 18%), then such doses may aid in weight reduction among this particular population. Tryptophan has not been reported to have consistent effects on hunger per se, and thus probably did not exert its effect by simply suppressing appetite among the three responders. Weinberger et al. (1978) found no reduction in food intake among food-deprived rats during the two hours after treatment with sufficient tryptophan (50 or 100 mg/kg) to raise brain tryptophan levels. Latham and Blundell (1979) observed a slight decrease in food intake among rats feeding freely on a single test diet, and no change in total daily food intake among food-deprived animals. The decrease in food intake resulted from a decrease in meal size and an increase in the between-meal interval.

The present results confirm and extend those described in our previous study on the effects of fenfluramine or tryptophan on carbohydrate snack intake by outpatients (Wurtman and Wurtman, 1981). In that study, subjects also monitored carbohydrate snack intake after treatment with tryptophan, fenfluramine, or their placebos. As in the present study, fenfluramine significantly diminished carbohydrate consumption in the group as a whole, and tryptophan significantly decreased carbohydrate intake in several individuals. In neither the prior nor the present study was tryptophan administered in the way most likely to enhance its brain intake, i.e., before meals and with some carbohydrate. Inasmuch as tryptophan's uptake from blood to brain is suppressed by the other LNAA in dietary proteins, it is possible that more of our subjects might have responded to tryptophan had it not been administered with protein-containing meals. The presence of a significant response in some individuals suggests that their obesity may be related to a disturbance in the mechanism coupling carbohydrate consumption to increases in brain serotonin synthesis. Conceivably, some individuals either release less-than-normal amounts of brain serotonin at any particular plasma Trp/LNAA ratio, or have a less-than-normal increase in this ratio after eating carbohydrate (e.g., because of insulin resistance). In either case, relatively larger proportions of dietary carbohydrate would be needed to produce normal increases in serotoninergic neurotransmission and thus to suppress appetite for carbohydrates. Since ingesting tryptophan, like eating carbohydrates, raises brain tryptophan, these subjects may have been able to reduce their carbohydrate snacking because the tryptophan, like dietary carbohydrate, accelerated serotonin synthesis.

The protocol used in this study allowed obese subjects to consume carbohydrate or protein snacks whenever they wished, and allowed the investigators to assess the value of specific drugs on the consumption of specific macronutrients (protein and carbohydrate). The relative rejection of the protein snacks and frequent consumption of carbohydrate snacks by our subjects indicate that some obese people do not simply overeat any food, but select particular foods to satisfy particular appetites. This finding suggests that the treatment of obesity should include evaluation of the patient's food intake patterns before beginning diet therapy, and determination of whether he or she consumes *all* food in excess or only certain macronutrients. Moreover, the times during which the subject is most likely to overeat certain types of foods should be known in order to develop diet plans that allow the dieter to satisfy a craving for particular foods when he or she is most likely to want them. If the dieter cannot control intake of specific foods like carbohydrate-rich snacks, anorectic drugs that decrease cravings for these foods could be incorporated into the treatment. Since the desire for such foods is not distributed equally over the entire day, the drugs can be reserved for administration before the period when consumption of the snacks is most likely to occur. This method of treatment may slow the development of drug tolerance and may also better treat the patient's specific appetite disturbance.

We thank Dr. William Rand for advice in statistical analysis; Dr. Joseph Hirsch for preparing the test drugs; the Seiler Corp. (Waltham, MA) for assistance in obtaining food supplies and a vending machine; Star Markets, Inc. (Cambridge, MA) for a donation; and the MIT Housing Office for assistance in arranging housing for the test subjects.

REFERENCES

Blundell, J. E.; Latham, C. J.; Moniz, E.; McArthur, R. A.; and Rogers, P. J. (1979). Structural analysis of the actions of amphetamine and fenfluramine on food intake and feeding behavior in animals and in man. *Curr. Med. Res. Opin.* (Suppl 1) 6:35–53.

Carlsson, A., and Lindqvist, M. (1978). Dependence of 5-HT and catecholamine synthesis on precursor amino-acid levels in rat brain. *Naunyn Schmiedebergs Arch. Pharmacol.* 303:157–164.

Fernstrom, J. D., and Wurtman, R. J. (1971). Brain serotonin content: increase following ingestion of carbohydrate diet. *Science* 174:1023–1025.

Fernstrom, J.D., and Wurtman, R. J. (1972a). Elevation of plasma tryptophan by insulin in the rat. *Metabolism* 21:337–342.

Fernstrom, J. D., and Wurtman, R. J. (1972b). Brain serotonin content: physiological regulation by plasma neutral amino acids. *Science* 178:414–416.

Fernstrom, J. D.; Wurtman, R. J.; Hammarstrom-Wilklund, B.; Rand, W. M.; Munro, H. N.; and Davidson, C. S. (1979). Diurnal variations in plasma concentrations of tryptophan, tyrosine, and other neutral amino acids: effect of dietary protein intake. *Am. J. Clin. Nutr.* 32:1912–1922.

Fuller, R.; Snoddy, R.; and Hemrick, S. (1978). Effects of fenfluramine and norfenfluramine on brain serotonin metabolism in rats. *Proc. Soc. Exp. Biol. Med.* 157:202–205.

Kyriakides, M., and Silverston, E. T. (1979). Comparison of the effects of d-amphetamine and fenfluramine on hunger and food intake in man. *Neuropharmacology* 18:1007–1008.

Latham, J. L., and Blundell, J. E. (1979). Evidence for the effect of tryptophan on the pattern of food consumption in free-feeding and food-deprived rats. *Life Sci.* 24:1971–1978.

Lewis, B. E. (1980). A Multiple Predictor Approach to Body Weight Regulation, Ph.D. dissertation, Clark University, Worcester, MA.

New York Metropolitan Life Insurance Co. (1959). New weight standard for men and women. *Statistical Bulletin* 40, pp. 1–4.

Pardridge, W. M. (1977). Regulation of amino acid availability to the brain. In Wurtman, R. J., Wurtman, J. J. (eds.), *Nutrition and the Brain.* New York: Raven Press.

Smith, S., and Saunders, C. (1969). Food cravings, depression and premenstrual problems. *Psychosomatic Med.* 31:281–287.

Weinberger, S.; Knapp, S.; and Mandell, A. (1978). Failure of tryptophan load induced increases in brain serotonin to alter food intake in the rat. *Life Sci.* 22:1595–1602.

Wool, I. G. (1965). Relations of effects of insulin on amino acid transport and on protein synthesis. *Fed. Proc.* 24:1060–1070.

Wooley, O.; Wooley, S.; and Lee, J. (1979). The effects of fenfluramine on appetite for palatable food in humans. *Curr. Med. Res. Opin.* (Suppl 1) 6:83–90.

Wurtman, J. J., and Wurtman, R. J. (1977). Fenfluramine and fluoxetine spare protein consumption while suppressing caloric intake by rats. *Science* 198:1178–1180.

Wurtman, J. J., and Wurtman, R. J. (1979). Drugs that enhance central serotoninergic transmission diminish elective carbohydrate consumption by rats. *Life Sci.* 24:895–904.

Wurtman, J. J., and Wurtman, R. J. (1981). Suppression of carbohydrate consumption as snacks and at mealtime by dl-fenfluramine or tryptophan. In Garattini, S. (ed.), *Anorectic Agents: Mechanisms of Actions, and of Tolerance.* New York: Raven Press.

Wurtman, R. J.; Hefti, R.; and Melamed, E. (1981). Precursor control of neurotransmitter synthesis: clinical implications. *Pharm. Rev.* 32:315–335.

Nutrients that Modify Brain Function

Richard J. Wurtman, M.D.

(From *Scientific American*, April 1982)

WHEN PEOPLE EAT, the concentration in their blood plasma of most amino acids (and of other food constituents) changes predictably in ways that depend on what foods are eaten. For people who take their meals at the usual times plasma amino acid levels generally exhibit pronounced daily rhythms. For example, among people consuming the high-protein diet typical of the United States the plasma concentration of the amino acid leucine is twice as high between 3:00 P.M. and 3:00 A.M. as it is during the rest of the day. If the same people eat protein-free meals, the leucine level instead falls by half during these hours of active digestion and absorption. In the first case the increase represents the entry into the bloodstream of some of the leucine in the dietary protein. In the second case the decrease results from the secretion of insulin (induced by ingested carbohydrate), which accelerates the passage of leucine and most other amino acids from the circulation into skeletal muscle.

My associates and I discovered these rhythmic, food-induced variations in the plasma level of various nutrients about a decade ago. We wondered whether the changes might have any functional significance. In particular we wondered whether the fluctuations in the concentration of circulating nutrients had any effect on the rate at which the nutrients are converted into cellular constituents. In order for changes in the level of a nutrient to influence the rate of conversion, the enzyme catalyzing the conversion must have a certain property. The enzyme's ability to bind the nutrient preparatory to changing its chemical structure must be relatively poor, so that at the usual nutrient concentrations each enzyme molecule is less than fully saturated with the nutrient and functions at less than peak efficiency. In this situation the quantity of the nutrient available to the enzyme is the rate-limiting element in the reaction, and so an increase in the nutrient's concentration increases the level of enzyme activity: more of the nutrient is converted and more of the product is formed.

We knew that tryptophan is converted into serotonin by just such a low-affinity enzyme. The release of serotonin by neurons originating in the brain stem delivers signals to widely scattered groups of neurons that control such things as sleep, mood, and appetite. Other investigators had already shown that the concentration of serotonin in the brain can be increased by giving experimental animals very large doses of pure tryptophan. John D. Fernstrom and I decided to examine the possibility that normal daily variations in the plasma concentration of tryptophan might be enough to alter the rate of serotonin synthesis in the rat brain. We found that even low doses of tryptophan, which raise the plasma concentration of the amino acid but keep it within the normal daily range we had previously established, did indeed enhance serotonin synthesis.

To see whether a reduction in plasma tryptophan had the opposite effect we injected some rats with insulin and gave others a diet of carbohydrates, which induces the secretion of insulin. We expected that the hormone would reduce the plasma level of tryptophan as it does that of other amino acids by moving them out of the bloodstream and into skeletal muscle. To our surprise the insulin did not lower the tryptophan concentration in the plasma, and it actually raised the concentration in the brain, increasing serotonin synthesis instead of reducing it. Feeding the animals large amounts of protein brought another surprise: even though amino acids were plentiful in the diet, both the brain concentration of tryptophan and the synthesis of serotonin were reduced.

The apparent paradoxes were resolved when we found that the amount of tryptophan available in the brain for conversion into serotonin depends not only on the amount of tryptophan in the plasma but also on the ratio of plasma tryptophan to the plasma level of five other amino acids: tyrosine, phenylalanine, leucine, isoleucine, and valine. All six of these amino acids are comparatively large molecules, and in a physiological environment most of them are electrically neutral, with about as much positive charge as negative.

It is very difficult for large, water-soluble molecules to diffuse out of the capillaries of the brain and gain access to neurons and other brain cells. Their passage between the blood and the brain is facilitated by carrier molecules present in the endothelial cells lining brain capillaries. A single species of carrier molecule transports all six of the large, neutral amino acids across the blood-brain barrier; the amino acids compete with one another for attachment to the carrier and hence for uptake from the bloodstream into the brain. There is far less tryptophan in most proteins than there is tyrosine, phenylalanine, leucine, isoleucine, or valine. A high-protein meal therefore reduces the plasma ratio of tryptophan to the competing amino acids; less tryptophan is carried across the barrier and less reaches the neurons.

A high-carbohydrate meal has the opposite effect because the insulin secreted in response to carbohydrate intake reduces the plasma level of the competing amino acids more than it does that of tryptophan. Whereas the other amino acids circulate as free molecules, most of the tryptophan is bound to the plasma protein albumin; segregated in an albumin reservoir, the tryptophan is essentially immune to the effect of insulin. The result is that after carbohydrates are eaten the plasma ratio of tryptophan to its competitors rises, causing more tryptophan to reach the neurons (see "Nutrition and the Brain" by John D. Fernstrom and Richard J. Wurtman; *Scientific American,* February 1974).

We proposed that these interactions enable the serotonin-releasing neurons in the brain to serve as sensors of the plasma tryptophan ratio, which increase serotonin release after a carbohydrate meal and reduce it after a high-protein meal. David Ashley and G. Harvey Anderson of the University of Toronto Faculty of Medicine subsequently found evidence that the brain exploits this property of the serotoninergic neurons when an animal chooses one food in preference to another. In an effort to define the specific food constituents whose choice is influenced by brain serotonin, Judith J. Wurtman and I allowed rats to choose between two diets having different proportions of carbohydrate and protein. Various treatments that increase serotonin release in the brain (such as giving the drug fenfluramine) caused the rats to selectively reduce their consumption of carbohydrate. Recently we have shown that serotonin-increasing treatments have a similar effect on obese people with a craving for dietary carbohydrate when they are allowed to choose from a range of snack foods over a period of several weeks.

It appears, in other words, that eating a meal rich in carbohydrate and poor in protein generates a neurochemical change — namely increased serotonin synthesis — that causes the animal to reduce its intake of carbohydrate but not of protein. It seems likely that this control of serotonin release by diet composition and of diet composition by serotonin release evolved because it helps to sustain nutritional balance. Presumably it keeps the bear from eating only honey and keeps human beings from eating sweets and starches to the exclusion of enough protein. Some obese people may suffer from a disturbance of this remarkable feedback mechanism that interlinks nutritional, metabolic, neurochemical, and behavioral systems. Unfortunately there is no noninvasive technique for measuring serotonin release in the brain and thus directly establishing the role of serotonin release in man.

Index

235

Tryptophan, *cont.*
  hunger and, 4–6, 8, 12, 52
Tuna Fish
  Casserole, 100
  Sandwich, 86–87

Vacations, dieting and,
  171–73
Vegetables, 85, 92–93, 114,
  120–21
  Meat, Rice, and, 128
  as nibbling foods, 153
Vitamins A and C, 49, 74,
  76

Weight
  desirable, for men ages 25
and over, 38
desirable, for women ages
  25 and over, 39
fat vs. water, 33–34,
  174–75
loss, exercising to accelerate, 176–80
loss, expected, on Carbo-
  hydrate Craver's Diet,
  34–36
loss, slowing down of,
  174–76
Weight Watchers frozen
  dinners, 106–7
Winter Salad, 87–88

Zinc, 12
Zipper test, 37